BASIC YANKEE

BASIC YANKEE

Steve Sherman

ARCO PUBLISHING, INC.
NEW YORK, N.Y.

All photographs were taken by the author

Published by Arco Publishing, Inc.
215 Park Avenue South, New York, N.Y. 10003

Library of Congress Cataloging in Publication Data

Sherman, Steve, 1938–
    Basic Yankee.

    1. New England—Social life and customs. 2.
Handicraft—New England. 3. New England—
Biography. 4. Interviews—New England. 5. New
England—Occupations. I. Title.
F10.S54   1984   306'.0974   84-9345
ISBN 0-688-05889-7 (Cloth Edition)

Printed in the United States of America

10 9 8 7 6 5 4 3 2 1

Contents

Acknowledgments

Many interested people helped with this book, including Linda Morley, New Hampshire State Folklorist, Michael Bell, Rhode Island State Folklorist, Neal Clark, writer and naturalist, Richard Kathman, director of the Canterbury Shaker Village, and as always Julia Older, who makes it all worthwhile and fun.

Preface

I thoroughly enjoyed my visits with these men and women of New England, and I came away reassured. In their quiet way they showed me that they're still thinking and doing basic Yankee.

But what's Yankee? It's a tough word to define. Yankee could be the direct-line descendants of English Puritan settlers on the first boat to the New World in the early 1600s. If only these are Yankee, then what about the French, Germans, Greeks, Irish, Poles, Finns, and the others who mingled in and contributed so much over the centuries? Just summer folk who winter over?

More than 12 million New Englanders live in six states of the northeast region, but how do you nail down which ones are real Yankees? The old joke tells the tale: To a European a Yankee is an American. To an American, a Yankee is a New Englander. To a New Englander, he is a Vermonter. To a Vermonter, he is someone who eats apple pie for breakfast. And to a Vermonter who eats apple pie for breakfast a Yankee is someone who eats it with a knife.

Someone else is always the Yankee. To a log-cabin man in central Maine the Cabots might be Yankee. To a Cabot blueblood in Back Bay Boston a real Yankee might be one of those Down-Easters with colonial plumbing. To which the Down-Easter would reply, yep, that might be right—Boston is too far away to amount to anything anyway.

To be sure, every true-blood Yankee has heard:

> Use it up
> Wear it out
> Make it do
> Or do without

A basic Yankee might be described as: thrifty, taciturn, independent, inventive, shrewd, private. Then again, is stubbornness merely a sign of unforgiveness? Is independence an excuse to be ornery? Does self-reliance disguise an unadventuresome nature? Who knows? Maybe Yankeeism is encapsulated in the words of one New Englander that *Yankee* magazine editor Jud Hale once quoted: "Why travel when I'm already here?"

Yankee is New England and New England is Emerson, Thoreau, Hawthorne, the Alcotts, Boston (the Athens of America), Peterborough Public Library (first tax-supported free library in the world), an extraordinary number of national leaders, a countryside of rare comforting beauty, the craggy inlets of Maine, the White Mountains of New Hampshire, the sugar maples of autumn in Vermont, the enticing sands of Cape Cod, Massachusetts, the lolling farms of Connecticut, the alluring Narragansett Bay of Rhode Island, the silent snowy nights, and the post-winter exuberance of green spring.

When it comes down to it, Yankee is more than a place. It's a continental state of mind. It's a coming home for all of us because our nation was born and bred in New England thinking and doing. Some of this thinking and doing are in these pages and that is what is reassuring. It's still going on.

These women and men do not sing their names and personalities in the limelight. They sing their thoughts and are what they do and have done. They are sugarers and lobstermen, boatbuilders and farmers, dowsers and auctioneers. Most of all, they are valuable because of their values. They are important because by learning through them what our fathers and founders sought we understand more of ourselves.

BASIC YANKEE

WILLIS JOHNSON

Ice Cutting

Willis Johnson

Hancock, New Hampshire

When Willis Johnson says that he wouldn't trade 15 minutes of his life for what young people are doing today, he means just that. "You do it your way, I'll do it my way," he says in his full-force, husky-timbered voice, the kind that lets you know he decided this long ago.

A strong, tall man of the outdoors, a loner-in-the-woods, Willis built 10 or 12 houses in Hancock (he can't remember how many exactly), some big, some small. The one he built for himself can only be described as one that Henry David Thoreau would like to have built himself. It's cozy, highly efficient, clean, neat as a pin. Not a thing out of place. A legless wood table he built is attached permanently to one wall. Saves space. A room divider he invented is on wheels; he calls this his movable wall so that when he wants to change the size of his bed-wide bedroom and front room he wheels the wall to where he wants it. Windows overlook nothing but well-kept forest and straightforward solitude. Of course, he dug his own well, and, of course, he built the highly skilled, finely executed fieldstone chimney that rises behind his black-iron Franklin stove. He cuts his own cordwood for heat and stacks it outside trimmer than a painting.

He's lived in Hancock all his 75 years, except during World War II. His grandfather George built a still-standing house at a sawmill he bought nearby in 1890. Later on Willis cut ice at the mill pond for his father Fred and for others elsewhere around the area.

In the first half of the century, ice was important for keeping food through the summer months. In those days people had to prepare well ahead of time, and cutting ice in winter provided refrigeration six months later.

1

In his green flannel shirt, blue jeans, and work shoes, Willis talks of ice cutting in the old days. He sits in one of three chairs in his cabin-castle. First, he takes out a black-framed photo that shows him in the 1930s maneuvering an ice-cutting machine on a frozen pond. He points to the photo and says in self-analysis, "Look at that goddamn cigarette."

What would be the typical size of a field of ice you'd cut?

Well, suppose somebody wanted 1,000 cakes. I used to cut at least 1,000 cakes some days up on Norway Pond in town. I cut ice on that pond at two and three o'clock in the morning. It never really gets dark, you know. There can be no moon at all, but it never really gets dark if there are no clouds. Well, the cakes were 16 inches square, so figure it out.

Did you make lines or just figure it out by sight?

I just figured out where the field was going to be, go over to the edge, and drop the saw down. And as you pull you get a line back of it. The saw fed itself. I was backing up. So you cut the ice and then it was easy to get a 90-degree. Once you go to the end of it, you do the cross cut.

How big a blade did you use?

Three feet in diameter. There's only 18 teeth on it. I built it myself. Now, the library had a book on motorcycles. Christ, I went to the library and got that book out endlessly on motorcycles. That's how I got acquainted so that I could build an ice saw.

In those days they cut ice with a plow pulled by horses. The knives were a foot long and they cut a foot deep. You go back and forth, back and forth, in the same groove until you got down. It was endless, long, slow work.

Tinkering with engines, hell, I figured I could do something myself. Before I got one perfected, I built three. The first one I built I used a Model T automobile engine. I didn't think a motorcycle engine would be powerful enough. A Model T. God, that was a clumsy rig.

2

He takes out a black-framed photo that shows him in the 1930s maneuvering an ice-cutting machine on a frozen pond. He points to the photo and says in self-analysis, "Look at that goddamn cigarette."

WILLIS JOHNSON   3

An old machinist in Peterborough helped me out a lot. The old guy took a differential and put an arbor through it. The arbor is what the sawblade is on. We cut off the housing on both sides of the differential. There was just the gears in there with the bearings. But the whole thing was very, very heavy. *Very* heavy. And also I used a wood sawblade that I fixed over pretty much, but it never worked good.

The next year I went to work using a motorcycle engine and wood frame, the main body. Things don't hold together with wood the way they do with steel. But I used that one on the mill pond. Well, it worked. So the next year I built one using a motorcycle engine. Then the year after that I built this one. It was steel. I spent a lot of time on it.

It must have taken a lot of time to figure out.

Well, it did. See [pointing to the photo], that's part of the motorcycle frame, and that's part of the motorcycle transmission. Everything was chain drive. I had to have some machine work done on it so I got on my motorcycle, I was riding a motorcycle then, I'd go to Peterborough to get the old machinist to work on it. My old man, he got madder than hell, you know. I was working for him, but I'd just take off. I heard since that he and my mother had words about it, but she said, "Leave him alone!"

You were very inventive. It's good to hear about people like you. And the saw worked all right. How long would it take to cut a thousand cakes?

Oh, two or three hours, that's all.

But other people used to do it with horses?

They did it with horses back and forth, back and forth. It took a long time. Hell, before that they had just the handsaws, you know. Long handsaws. It was very slow.

How long did it take with horses?

I don't remember. I remember doing it with horses. It seemed endless. We started in cutting ice in the morning, one horse that's what you used, and you worked the horse all day pretty much.

ICE CUTTING

One year in town here they had very thin ice, *very* thin ice. The ice on the pond got so thin nobody dared go out on it. But the old reservoir was up there and they got permission from the town so they got me to go up there to cut ice for them.

How much would somebody have to pay for a thousand ice cakes?

Well, I cut it for a cent a cake, that's what I cut it for. Ten bucks. Ten bucks in those days was damn good money, you know.

It was. What was the best time to cut the ice?

What you did was watch it. And that was always after the first of January. That's when it got thicker.

It had to be at least 16 inches?

Yeah, well, that worked out the best. With thin ice they probably cut it less than that. Most of the stuff I cut, they waited a little to get it thicker. Then they went right to work on it until everybody got their icehouses full. Once they got started, that was it, period. That was the job.

Willis comes from a family of long life. His Hancock-born father Fred lived 82 years, his mother Mary Miller, born in New Brunswick, Canada, 86, his grandmother, 93. He was part of a family of four boys and three girls. As he tells it, his brothers and sisters "all knew what the word work meant." As for his father, he gives no better epitaph than what early New England demanded of its people: "He worked for himself and made a good living off the land."

Willis gets up to answer the phone, talks awhile. He stands, looking out the window. Then he hangs up and says with a grin, "One of my women." Mary Hibbard. He tells how they get together about once a week to talk and eat. He tells how she takes care of other people in town, such as a woman with multiple sclerosis, an old Army colonel who's alone, a woman who just had an eye operation. "She's got a heart as big as a globe," he says, describing how she calls him up every day or two to see how he is. "She's a pretty good person," he says.

———————————

So what did the people do? They came down to the ponds and loaded up their trucks?

Yep.

How large would a typical icehouse be?

Well, it depended on how much ice you wanted. The walls were built thick, double walls, and they filled them with sawdust.

For insulation.

Yeah. And the ice was packed in there in a single block, one single block. You laid a tier and then another tier and another. Once it was full then it was completely buried in sawdust.

It wouldn't melt together into a big chunk?

That's right, it wouldn't. The more it was together the longer the ice would last. See what I mean? It wouldn't melt enough to stick together. The blocks'd break away from one another. Because when you put it in there, there's no water. Everything is froze. With no water it's not going to melt together. Once it was filled, it was buried, period.

How high a block would it be?

Depends. I remember we put some 14-, 15-, 16-foot square inside. I think we piled it there about 8 feet high, one single big block. That's a lot of ice. That's a *hell* of a lot of ice. Nothing in there but ice and sawdust. You chipped it out of there, washed it, and put it in a refrigerator. The refrigerator, you lifted up the top and put the ice down in the top. And there was a dish underneath the refrigerator in one corner and the water ran into it from the ice. It had to be emptied every day or the floor'd be covered with water. Overflow, you know. But you had to wash off the sawdust. Hell, that was one of the chores we had to do as kids.

Was it enough to last through August?

You put enough in there and it'd last through summer. That was the idea. Experience taught them how much they had to have to go through the summer.

You cut ice here in town most of the time. Anywhere else?

Well, yeah, as time went on, at Zephyr Lake in Greenfield, a big icehouse down there. A hell of a big building. It burned when I was in the service, I guess. The Whiting Milk Company in Boston, that was their icehouse. The Boston and Maine Railroad came through and this was ice that went in refrigerator cars by the carload. Every day. They shipped ice into Boston every day.

Well, they had a winter of thin ice down there and they lost the saw in the pond. The ice was only about 8 or 10 inches thick.

How big was the saw that went through?

It was a very heavy rig. Four cylinder engine. It took three or four men to run it. It must've weighed 1,000 or 1,200 pounds.

How much did yours weigh?

It probably weighed a couple hundred pounds. I had a Model A Ford roadster with the back cut out and a platform built in there. I dragged that thing up on it myself, no trouble at all. I weighed 190 though. I was no baby then.

So you went down to Zephyr Lake.

Yeah, they heard of me, they got me down there. They gave me a blade. They gave me 90 dollars and board and room and everything. That was damn good money in those days, Christ.

WILLIS JOHNSON   7

'Course, I worked from five o'clock in the morning until ten o'clock at night. They had a hell of a big crew there and they were putting in a hell of a lot of ice. It was an endless operation. The train came through there every day.

They lost a pair of horses in the pond, too. I saw a pair go down. One of them died right there and I think they had to shoot the other one. That was horrible.

How did you plot out the field?

Wherever the ice was thick, I'd drop the blade in there to see how deep it was. Then I cut a channel through the thin ice 3 or 4 inches thick. I could set the rig to cut at different heights. It'd feed itself. I had one hand on it to keep it going straight, right out there in front. I was afraid I was going to go right into the pond.

How would you get the ice out of the pond?

Some men came with pipe poles and pushed the ice I cut onto the other ice they chipped out at an angle. They had tongs with long handles on them. You could stand up with them and grapple the ice. At the mill pond the old man built a platform over the dam and brought the ice up with a chain conveyer and put it in the icehouse.

It was a big business.

Oh, yeah, it was a hell of a business back in those days.

Then it stopped about the 1940s when electric refrigeration took over?

The last ice was cut on the mill pond about 1944. In the town history there are pictures with captions that ice was cut on that guy's pond. The last ice was cut in 1944 and we sold to that guy in 1958. Cutting ice on *his* place! That son of a bitch, I kicked him off my place, you know, kicked him off my land. Goddamn him, I kicked him off. He avoids me now. Never see him. I think if he sees me coming, even smells me, he's gone. It's a damn lie.

You could cut ice and store it today the same way, couldn't you?

I was thinking awhile back about cutting ice in the old days and the job of getting it off the pond. Why not build some forms and build them at a slight angle. You can get waterproof plywood today. Build some waterproof plywood forms. Or use some plastic basket or pails. And when we get this sub-zero weather, go out there at noontime and fill it up with water. The next day they should be solid blocks of ice, and then put them in your icehouse and bury them with sawdust. And fill them up again. One time we had a cold spell that lasted two weeks. Why couldn't a man freeze his own ice and put it away without having a pond?

Willis turns and points to a ridge where two black horses are buried. His father never traded them when their usefulness was gone. Willis took care of them, drove them through the woods, mowed hay with them, plowed with them, hauled stone with them. To him it was just like a man with his dog. No different. They were his life, he says.

When he got through working at night, whatever time it was, Willis went to the barn and let out the horses, Jack and Jerry, to relax, too. They stayed around him just like dogs.

One time Jerry, weighing about 1,800 pounds, got twisted off balance by another horse and stumbled over a log. He got Jerry unhitched finally, got him rolled over, and back on his feet again. But not before the big horse lay there with his feet up in the air and Willis just talking to him, "It's OK, Jerry, it's OK."

You liked your life overall.

I don't see why not. You see these kids today. Those kids are making big money. But I wouldn't trade 15 minutes of my time with them. Their thinking and the way they handle themselves. I wouldn't do it. You do it your way, I'll do it mine.

When kids get started, they got to borrow a lot of money. They got to pay that interest. Period. We weren't strapped that way. I was brought up to have the same thinking as my dad. My dad never had a mortgage. If he bought a car, he paid for it right across the barrelhead. If he bought property, he paid for it. He never went to the bank. Just to 'put money in! I practice pretty much the same way.

What do you think is the difference in values between now and when you had to cut ice? Most people don't know how to do basic things like that now. Do you think it makes people less inventive when they have to rely on so many other people more?

Today they really don't want to put the time into thinking that they might be able to handle the situation themselves. Really, I think that's what's wrong. My dad had seven kids and he really couldn't afford to hire a millwright. He had to do it himself. And he was sawing out stock. He had to take care of his own saws. It wouldn't have cost near as what it costs today, but he still wouldn't have a man come and do this and that. He did it himself!

I don't know how my brothers and sisters thought about it, but I spent a lot of time with him. I started working with him when I was 15 years old and until I was 30. He was my teacher. I don't know how much I am today, but he made me what I am. He really did. Without question. I wouldn't be the guy I am without my old man. It was good to get away from him when I did, but I learned something from him.

You learned a lot.

Yeah, a lot. I could have learned lot more about people than I did. But I don't know. I wouldn't want to change it. If I had a chance to go back and do it over again, I'd want to do the same thing again.

10   ICE CUTTING

ED BLACKMORE

Lobstering

Ed Blackmore

Stonington, Maine

In the early days the Dutch reported catching lobsters 6 feet long off the eastern coast and colonial diarists write of 25-pound lobsters on the dinner table. Ever since, lobster fishing and lobster eating have been two of the most prized activities in New England, especially in Maine. Ed Blackmore has fished for lobsters for 31 years out of Stonington, a working fishing town set on an isolated rocky peninsula jutting alongside Penobscot Bay.

Homarus americanus is as familiar to New Englanders as sugar maples and stone walls. These particular lobsters are known for their large pincer-like front claws, but more appreciated is the lobster meat, especially the tail. In the water lobsters are greenish, but once cooked they turn bright fire-engine red. Cooked, dipped in melted butter, and eaten plain, they're supreme, although more people probably know Lobster Newburg as the number one dish. This concoction, lobster meat in a cream-and-sherry-based sauce, was originally Lobster Wenberg, named after a customer of the famous Delmonico's restaurant in New York in the 1890s. When Wenberg got in a fight one night in the stylish restaurant, Delmonico changed the name to Newburg by switching some letters around.

Plain or fancy, delectable lobster eating begins with the hard work of lobster fishermen. Blackmore worked on his own in lobstering the hard way. He's now president and executive director of the 800-member Maine Lobstermen's Association and chairman of the Maine Lobster Advisory Council. He knows whereof he speaks.

In blue windjacket and red Association cap, he talks about his lobstering days and how they compare to today.

When you were starting out, how did you establish an area to fish?

Well, my grandfather was a lobsterman and he had an established area. I went with him as a high-school boy, helping him, and I went with my brother fishing. So I had all this experience in a given area, so to speak. When I got ready to go on my own, well, this is my area. I was challenged by a couple of people, but soon as they found out that I was serious about it and intended to stay, I didn't have any more problems.

What do you mean by "challenged" exactly?

When I started out on my own, I set out my traps where I figured I ought to fish. Occasionally, I'd have a trap cut or someone'd pull it up, you know, jump both feet into it, smash it up all to bits. It didn't take me too long to figure out who it was. You know, if you return what you get, why after awhile that don't go over too good either. It's no point beating up on me if they're going to have to suffer, too. If they find you're going to take it, you're in for it because they'll give as much as you'll take. Anytime they bother me with a trap or two, well, I'd. . . . I realize this isn't the way to do it, but this is the way you have to do it if you're going to survive.

You were protecting your territory.

Right. I didn't intend for them to drive me out or to steal my traps or cut them off.

Do lobstermen still have to do that to protect their territory today?

Yeah, but much more so in the eastern section. In the western section of the state those traditions have fallen by the wayside a little bit. But the more you get into the eastern section the more protective the fishermen are, because basically you're looking at a really different setup. You're looking at a coastal community, small, a lot of island people, and fishing is the only thing they have. So when the fish is gone, then they can't make a living. The tourists come in, buy their property, buy their homes, and first thing you know you've got a tourist community, it's no longer a fishing community. So all the fishermen are pretty protective of their area, whereas you go down along Portland and some of the more populated areas, well, you know, if you don't go fishing you can get a job ashore someplace, a factory, a mill, some kind of other employment. Down east a little bit there's no other employment. That's it.

Yes, that's understandable. How big an area did you personally fish?

I fished an area that ran seaward probably to 18 miles out to sea. The width coastwise was probably four miles wide. It wasn't exclusively mine, but this was the area that I fished. Even though I was in the area for 31 years, there were areas in close proximity that I couldn't fish. I guess if I wanted to make a real war out of it, you know, make a whole lot of trouble, I could have fished it. But it really wasn't worth it. I had enough area without fighting for another square mile or two. As long as those guys didn't move into my area, didn't hassle me, I wasn't going to move into theirs. We kind of had an unwritten understanding.

That's a large area. How many traps did you use?

I seldom ran over 400 traps. I worked with a helper the last ten or 15 years.

How often did you check them?

If the weather was good, I could check the 400 every day. If the weather wasn't too good, or I wasn't too good, I might haul 300, 350, and said I'll give those other 50 another night to set. So then I'd start in on them the next day. 'Course, the longer they set generally the better the catch is. So if I left a few over that'd kind of sweeten the pot the next day.

You know, in the summer it's daylight at four-thirty and doesn't get dark until eight or nine o'clock. I put in a day that I wouldn't get home till six-thirty, seven o'clock at night. I put in a long day. I didn't start with 400 traps either. When I started I probably started with 125, 130 traps. Had a little small boat, an old boat, kind of a leaky old boat. I just had to go with whatever I could afford. A small boat, a small string of traps, until I got that paying. Then I could afford a better boat.

What size boat did you end up with?

I ended up with a 35-foot Jonesport boat, diesel engine, loran, radar, all the good equipment.

With 400 traps what percentage had a catch in them?

Oh, Jesus, that would vary. I've hauled those 400 for 75 pounds of lobster, and I've hauled them for 600 pounds of lobsters. When they're not there, they're not trapping. Lobstering is something that when you set your gear and you don't get anything, that don't mean anything. That don't mean there's no lobsters there. The only time you catch a lobster is when they get ready for you to catch them! When he wants to feed, when he gets hungry. Now a lobster doesn't eat every night, sometimes only two or three nights. Of course, after they molt or shed their shell, they get their new shell, much bigger than the old one, it's not filled out with meat, and they're hungry, they start to go for the food. They catch much better then.

And the bait? What do you use?

They use a combination. A lot of fishermen like red fish rack, what's left when they bring in the draggings for the processing plant. They fillet the meaty section off and sell it on the market as a rose fish. You don't see it in New England much, it's marketed more in the Midwest. The frames that's left, you know, the heads and tails and bones and stuff, they go to waste. So they sell these racks to the lobstermen for bait. They use herring in the summertime, they either get those from the herring fishermen or get them from the sardine plants after the sardine plants take what they want. They cut off the head, they cut off the tail, and put the middle part in the can. The head and tail go to waste again, so the fishermen buy the waste from the sardine factory. Down this way a lot of fishermen will use porgies or menhaden.

16

Anytime you see a 2- or 3-pound lobster, he didn't get that big because he ran into the first trap he saw. He got big because he went around a whole lot of traps. He reached in and pulled out what he could get without going in. That's how he got big!

Sometimes lobsters'll like fresh bait, new bait; other times they like old bait. I always found that whatever you were using, whether you were using fresh bait or if you were using a lot of salt bait, almost anytime that you change the bait when you haul it'd be a little better. Lobsters are like anybody else: they get tired of eating the same old stuff. You give them a change, they'll go for that at least once, maybe twice. They don't run into the trap just because you put bait on it. They crawl over it, they crawl around it. Anytime you see a 2- or 3-pound lobster, he didn't get big because he ran into the first trap he saw. He got big because he went around a whole lot of traps. He reached in and pulled out what he could get without going in. That's how he got big!

What does it take to be a lobsterman? What are those certain characteristics, do you think?

'Course, a lobsterman will tell you it takes a strong back and a weak mind! Well, it sure as heck takes a strong back. This lobstering is a game you want to get in when you're 18 or 21 years of age and you want to work like hell for 15 or 20 years, take care of your equipment, take care of your money. Just because you make good money today don't think that if you blow it all you're going to make good money 25 years from now. Lot of things can happen to you. You can use yourself up physically. When you're 40, you're going downhill if you're a lobsterman, whether you admit it or not. You probably won't admit it when you're 40, but you admit it when you're 50. You damn well realize it when you're 50.

The worst thing that can happen to a lobster fisherman is if he's got a Chevy body with a Cadillac engine in it. He's sure going to destroy himself, because by the time he's 50 he could very well be all crippled up, pulled all out of joint. He could be the best patient in a chiropractor's office. You're much better off with a Cadillac body with a Chevrolet engine in it. Then you're in for the long haul, you'll make it through.

———

Usually lobstermen are highly independent, like most fishermen. Most of them fish the way they've fished for generation upon generation. The methods stay the same more or less. Areas are handed down from father to son and so are the ways of doing the catching. Lobstermen usually work alone, set their traps alone, and haul them up alone. When they do work with someone, which they call a sternman, it's often a son or a grandson or a son-in-law. Sometimes a lobsterman will take out his wife if the children are grown or away from home for some reason. They go out in shedding season, which starts about the middle of July and runs through December.

Blackmore remembers the biggest lobster he ever caught. It was about 15 or 16 pounds. "It couldn't even get into the trap," he says. "Damn big thing." He had to throw it back because it was over maximum legal size, that is, anything over 5 inches on the body measurement.

Why is there a maximum limit?

They've established to a reasonable degree that the big females hold a huge amount of eggs, and the scientists say that it takes a big male to breed a big female. The large female won't mate with a much smaller male. They prefer a lobster somewhere in the same size range. So we've left the big ones on the bottom. When you take a lobster the minimum size, 3¾16 inches, that lobster will carry about 16,000 eggs, but that lobster just over the maximum carries 75,000 eggs. So when she does her thing she does it in a big way. She's got that huge tail and all those seeds, she carries them under her tail. It takes about ten to 11 months for her to bring those eggs out from the inside. Then it takes about another eight or nine months that she carries them extruded under her tail before she releases them.

Is lobstering as good today as it was when you started out?

Not for the individual. By that I mean that the overall catch is quite high, but this is not an indication of how well everybody is doing. Because the number of traps has probably increased at least tenfold, something like that. So what we're really doing is slicing the pie thinner and thinner all the time. The industry is overcapitalized. Too damn many people in it, too many traps. It keeps getting harder and harder earning the same amount of money each year. Your operating expenses keep increasing, you have to fight harder and harder with your neighbor for your share of the catch. So individually it isn't good.

When I started with 150 traps, I was catching as many lobsters with those as I was with 400. There wasn't that much competition. One thing that's different today is that when a younger guy is ready, there's more ready money available. You can go to the bank and they'll loan you money to build a boat, get traps, that sort of thing. It sounds pretty good, but it's not good for the business. That's how it got overcapitalized. When I started in, you started in with your *own* money, you worked that up until it got a little better, you got a little better boat. Hell, it took me most of a lifetime to get a brand new boat. I never owned a brand new boat right out of the shop until I was almost 40. It was a first-class boat, but I was of the school that I wouldn't go into debt for 40,000 dollars. These young guys today, they go into debt for 40,000 dollars for a boat, 50,000 dollars for a house, another 12,000 dollars for a pickup truck. They wonder why they have to put out a thousand traps just to make the payments. It's a vicious circle that they're in. There's so much pressure on them to make the payments. They're working for the bankers all the time.

It must be a little disheartening for these values to change?

It is. Like some years ago, one of those hurricane storms came up the coast and destroyed a lot of traps and one thing or another. The government came out and offered some disaster loans for some fishermen. Totally wrong. Never should have happened. Some guys never had more than a handful of traps; they claimed they had 500, 600 traps, lost them all, then went to the government, got these disaster loans, never repaid them. Next year they come out with a brand new outfit, better than the guy who's been fishing all his life. Well, a group of us went to the Governor and told him we don't want any more asking for disaster loans for fishermen for traps.

You know, when you go fishing you accept the fact that you may lose your traps. You take care of these traps. Because there are places where you can place these traps where you won't lose them. If you put them in shallow water right up against the rocks, you're going to lose them when a storm comes. If a guy loses his boat, loses his wharf, something like that, help him out. But if he loses his traps, that's what you accept when you go lobstering.

What about the market? Is the market still good for lobsters? Is it better now than in your day?

The market is really good. It's better. There's no end to the market. We used to have times when we'd be having a glut of lobsters on the market at certain times of the year. But we see it very little now because the market has expanded, shipment methods are better. One thing we have to be careful though, is what I remember one time. When we went on strike when the price was too cheap, getting 25 cents a pound, we said we wouldn't go for that. We said we wanted a minimum of 30 cents. You could go to the supermarket and buy them retail for 39 cents. Oh, God, I said, this is bad. Lobsters are going to be a common supermarket item in the low-cost category. This is going to hurt us. I was wrong, totally wrong then. What this did, it had to happen, I guess, it allowed people who never tasted lobster before to taste it. It let a whole generation of people in on lobster. Well, once they got the taste then we were home free! If the price went up, they didn't care. If the price went up still, they still liked them.

With the price continuing to increase, the lobsterman himself doesn't get a big spin-off of price, but what we have to be careful of is that the retail price doesn't get so high it creates consumer resistance. If we take this taste of lobster away from a generation, we're not going to have the demand for our product. So we've got to be very careful that we don't price ourselves out of the market.

What about oil drilling offshore? Doesn't this affect lobstering?

We're concerned about this. Of course, the goddamn oil companies, they'll tell you what they want to tell you, what they think you ought to hear. They drill and dump sediment all over the bottom in the offshore area. I don't think there's any real extensive monitor of what the effect is. It's tough to fight the oil companies. They've got a lot of money and they control a lot of people in Washington. I think the State of Massachusetts has done as much as anybody. They've continually fought offshore drilling. Are we destroying the fisheries? The oil thing is invested in the short term. The oil isn't going to last. They're going to drill it, they're going to pump it, and they're going to get out. Whereas the fishing has been there and always will be there. It's a renewable resource.

Storms can be really dangerous to fishermen. Have you ever been in trouble 18 miles out?

Yeah, I've been in trouble 18 miles out. One time when I was a young fella I was out there in wintertime and it was getting along about three in the afternoon, gets dark at four, you know. Started shoveling fine snow, visibility was cutting down, the engine conked, we couldn't get it going. Jesus Christ, the wind's offshore. Are we going to spend the night out here adrift? We didn't have any stove or anything. Jesus, the snow was in and out, thickening up, then let up a little bit. 'Bout that time we spotted a boat down to the south of us. We just saw it. We didn't have no radio or anything at that time. What we did was that my brother was with me, and he got up on top of the pilothouse and took his jacket and waved it and the guys down there at the other boat happened to see us. They saw somebody waving at them and knew somebody was in trouble. So they towed us in, getting dark then, too, and we were pretty thankful.

After mining, fishing is the most dangerous occupation in the country. Every now and then a lobsterman gets his feet tangled in the line when setting a trap and gets pulled overboard. The boat will be circling around and around until somebody finds it. Sometimes they find the lobsterman, sometimes they don't. Sometimes a gasoline engine will leak, sparks ignite the gas, and a fire burns a boat and lobsterman out of the water. "Fishermen take a lot of chances," Ed says. " 'Well, it's good enough, good enough.' But sometimes it isn't good enough."

One time a lobsterman from Jonesport bent down to a faltering shaft and got his ragged jacket sleeve caught. It pulled him down so hard that it stalled the engine, broke his arm in six places, and he couldn't get loose for two and a half hours until somebody spotted him. He lost his arm.

Through it all Ed ended up as a charter member of the Maine Lobstermen's Association and a vocal, active member of federal and state agencies and commissions. He hasn't fished commercially for lobsters in five years, but he's proud that Stonington is returning as a rejuvenated lobster and fishing town.

What was your best year?

1957. I don't know the total count, but I know it was a damn good year. Lobsters started early and they hung on late. 'Course, I always fished over the winters. It was one of the few times I made anything in winter. Most times it was just swapping an old dollar for a new one, you know. That was one of the years, I think, that we had a number of hurricanes coming up the coast. Christ, we started with Ann and Betsy and Carol and Donna and Edith. Christ, we were halfway down the alphabet before the season was over, you know. It was good if you didn't have your gear around the rocks and have it all smashed up. Of course, I lost some gear, but I never was one to fish real close to rocks because I'd been through some of those experiences and lost quite a lot of gear. Even though I knew there was pretty good fishing near the rocks, I wouldn't put all my gear in there because it was a gamble. But it seemed like most storms kept the bottom stirred up and the lobsters hungry. Their natural food wasn't available to them or something. We had a real bad storm late in the fall and a lot of guys lost a lot of gear. Well, I didn't get hurt too bad. My brother, he didn't either. We put our gear together and set it offshore. First few times we hauled that gear you wouldn't believe how many lobsters we had.

With more than one lobster in a trap?

Oh, hell yes. The most lobsters I ever got in a trap, I'll tell you, was 21.

Twenty-one! In a regular-size trap?

Yeah, regular size. It might have been a 38-inch-size trap. Softwood trap. I'll tell you how I did it. I went out early in the morning and I hauled this trap. I got 14 count ones in there, the ones I could keep; there was other stuff in there, too, I had to throw out. I hauled all day long. At night I had to come right by this trap. Jesus, I said, that trap done some good in the morning, I'll haul that again, see what it's doing. I took seven out of it in the afternoon! So all told, I got 21 out of that trap in a day.

Terrific. You make your own traps?

Yeah, I always did. You got to work like hell if you're going to make three a day.

Did you use the same design trap as your grandfather?

No, grandfather used to have what we call the straight-headers. Hell, I'd seen him haul them things and they'd come up the side of the boat and a lobster was coming in one end and going out the other end. Well, after awhile, what we call the parlor trap came along. That's the trap you see today with the entrances on the side, then a big head in the middle and drops into the parlor. These traps were much more efficient than anything else previous to that. That design is still pretty good. It hasn't been improved too much.

Over the years did you change your methods much or did you fish pretty much the way you learned from your grandfather?

Well, I don't think I changed my methods. You get a lot smarter over the years. I could take a lot less traps and get more lobsters than somebody just coming into the industry. Because I learned that when there was lobsters over here there was lobsters over there at the same time. I learned that they were in certain depths of water, certain bottom types at the same time. In the summertime you're looking at two or three fathoms up to ten fathoms. When you get into winter fishing, you have to go deeper.

There were a lot who never fished in the winter because they never had the ability to fish in the winter. When you get offshore, you had to pick up land bearings and run a compass course and time it. If you didn't, you'd never find your gear when you got out there and the days are short. You had to know what the hell you were doing. You just couldn't go out there and sail around an hour or two looking for your traps, and time is money. A lot of guys just never developed the ability to do this.

It's different today. They just run their gear off loran and write the number down. Makes a fisherman out of everybody. Everybody's a fisherman today. You had to learn to be a fisherman years ago.

Do most of the lobstermen abide by the size limits?

We have a few renegades like anything else, but the serious lobstermen abide by it. They know that this is their future. They don't abide by it and bring in the shorts, they're cheating themselves next year. You only catch them once, you know. But the worst problem, I think, is the people who aren't serious fishermen, who have another job to go to. The ones who have 50 or 75 traps and a cottage or some damn thing. They bring in shorts, so what? They get caught, they take their license, they still got a job. Whereas if a lobsterman gets caught, he loses his license, he's out of business. His livelihood is gone. He doesn't have any other way to make his livelihood. So he's more careful he doesn't get involved in that sort of thing.

Now here's the big question. What's the very best way to cook lobster?

The best way to cook a lobster? Well, I've had them boiled and baked and stuffed with crab meat and melted butter and something on top of that. Jesus Christ, they're out of this world. But when you talk about boiled lobster, you go to one of these places and see a big kettle of water. They put the lobsters in a bag or something and immerse them into the water. This is not the way to get the best lobster. The best lobster, if you're going to keep the taste, is to *steam* the lobster. You use about 2 inches of water, no more, maybe a little less, then put a little salt in. Saltwater is definitely a plus. Then put the lobster in. Let the steam come up through the lobster. If you immerse them in water, you're sucking out some of the goodness. They look the same and everything, but the steamed lobster, for my money, is *much* better than one that's been boiled.

LEO CORMIER

Maple Sugaring

Leo Cormier

Hancock, New Hampshire

The day we go out to Leo Cormier's sugar orchard the sky is partly cloudy and granite boulders are bulging through the low snow. Leftover beech leaves are fluttering and make the only noise. Leo wears a black and red plaid cap, green work pants, wide-bearing suspenders, a hefty insulated jacket, and Maine boots with rubber bottoms and leather tops (good for mud season). He runs a middling-size operation and taps about 400 trees, although he gets sap from 600 taps since some big trees take three and four taps each.

Like many others, he collects the sap in barrels, transfers it to a gathering tank, trucks it three miles on country roads to his sugarhouse behind his home, pipes it through his evaporator, boils it off with wood fire, jugs it, and seals it. It's basically the same way people like him have been sugaring for generations.

Authentic maple syrup is the *crème de la crème* of sweeteners, the champagne of New Hampshire, one of the supreme products of nature. Nothing can beat the true stuff. No chemical corn syrup substitute for Leo Cormier. No paraformaldehyde tablets in the tapholes to speed up the flow and get into the sap. Leo worked at sugaring when he was a youngster and he's doing it again now. It's hard work, long hours, and taxing on patience, but when the sugar snow comes (the last spring snow) maple sugaring time waits for nobody.

The sap runs on a schedule of cold nights and warm days. Leo looks for wet and cold weather, snow or rain, frosty night. A day around 35 degrees with a southeast wind starts the sap running upward to resurrect the branches from winter rest. We stand at one end of his orchard. It's not a large one, not small, just the kind you'd expect from this 69-year-old man. Only the maple trees show. All

29

the underbrush and pines have been cleared out. More hard work. This way the sunlight can get in to warm the maples faster and better. Also, the maples aren't fighting the other roots for moisture.

Leo uses flexible plastic tubing that runs from tree tap to tree tap into blue plastic 50-gallon barrels. His operation is big enough and steady enough for this instead of picking up individual buckets and transferring them to a central barrel.

———————

Have you always done it with tubing?

No, as a boy I done it on the family farm in Dalton, New Hampshire. We pulled it all in with horses. We had buckets. You put the team right out through the woods there. You got as close as you could. Then you lugged it in with two big 5-gallon pails with a yoke or on snowshoes, whatever. We used to run about 1,500 taps up there on top of a mountain. Pulled it all in with horses.

Let's hope you had a lot of brothers and sisters.

I was the last one home. I was the one got hooked with it. My mother would do the boiling. We had a 3 × 12 evaporator up there. I'd go up to gather, she'd boil. She come home about one o'clock at night, you know. She had cataracts in both eyes. She couldn't see more than 5 or 6 feet. She'd come down off the mountain with a lantern in her hand.

She sounds like a good hardy woman. How much did you make then?

Oh, around 100 gallons, I guess. We sold it to get extra money for taxes and stuff like that. Back then you sold a gallon for around 3 dollars, three fifty. That was just before Depression.

So there was a time when you didn't do any sugaring.

Then I got the feeling of kind of wanting to do it. Then Johnny Robinson loaned me a little evaporator, 2 × 4, Johnny

Robinson over in Greenfield. Over there talking one day. "Gee, I got me an itch to do some sugaring. Got nothing to work with." "How would you like a little 2 × 4 to start off with?" He loaned me everything to do it with. That's how I started up here.

It's not a profitable thing. It's a lot of work for what you get out of it. It's for extra cash. You pay taxes or something like that. You figure your time you wouldn't make a nickel an hour. [Holds up tubing with bubbles going through] You shoulda been down here yesterday. See that there. Them things were just going crazy. I get the biggest kick out of them, watching them go.

You can hear it, too.

Hear it going there.

It's all by gravity, I take it.

All gravity. It's closed circuit. Tight circuit.

How many feet of tubing do you think you have?

Each line has about 500 and 600 feet. I get five lines in here. I don't go with the big manifold line with an inch tubing. I didn't want to go that elaborate. I've done all right this way, it's worked well for me.

You got to walk your line, make sure there's no leak. If there's a leak halfway down, you're not going to get any sap. It's going to stop at that point.

So you have to see that the bubbles are going through.

Watch them. Soon's I get a chance I'll walk every line when they're running and carry my pail and repairs with me. If you need to make a repair, you make it right then and there. I've made a few. Yeah, you have to. Squirrels'll get into them. I haven't had too much trouble this year. Last year! Oh, they just about murdered me. Every time I come in, see one that wasn't running. All you got to do is start walking back and you know you find that leak. You find a place in the snow where the water's been dripping, you got a leak there.

How many taps can a tree take? I heard that they can take just about any reasonable number. Is that true?

Well, you try to keep them down, depending on the size of the tree. Well, this tree here, 2 feet through maybe, I got two taps on it. I don't get too rugged on them. You know, you're tapping them every year. Some guys'll put three or four on there. Well, that's a little bit rank, you know. So I go a little lighter.

You usually like to hit the southeast side, you get your best run. You tap it over on this north side, well, it ain't going to run till later. When the others are done, this side of the tree is going to be running. The south side. It warms up faster. The sun's hitting it.

How do you know when to come out here? When's the right time?

Well, watch the weather. If it warms up, gets up to 40, it's halfway decent, you know they're running, if the night was cold before. They ain't got to, but more than likely they're going to. I picked up three barrels this morning. I thought there'd be more. I just bring my tractor in here, load up, and I'm gone.

You see, they're still running. They were stopping when I come up, but it warmed up just a notch. A slight variation in the weather. Evidently, it's clouding in, it's getting a little warmer, because the sun's gone over.

Trees are very sensitive to the weather, aren't they?

Very sensitive. I seen them when they'd be stopped. Just like we're talking here, they start right up.

You number the lines. See this tag. You got to make every corner. It's got to be exact or else your spokes aren't going to come right. I got a mark on the tree. You mark the tree. See that tree there. Number 7, number 8, number 10 over there. You start from that point and you follow the arrow on the tree, which side you want to be, just a little yellow paint. See that point there? Just make an X. You got to follow every crook. You miss one and you're in trouble. I know last year I made a wrong corner. I bet you I was three hours getting that thing straightened out! Yeah.

. . . this tree here, 2 feet through maybe, I got two taps on it. I don't get too rugged on them. You know, you're tapping them every year. Some guys'll put three or four on there. Well, that's a little bit rank, you know.

Leo has an infectious grin and laugh. He laughs at the fun of it all, talking about the dribbling sap and the infernal mistakes he makes now and then. He talks in a clipped New Hampshire way, a man of the woods and nature where economy and friendliness have their equal share. He likes to talk and he likes what he does. He's lived in Hancock since 1957.

He taps on three heavily wooded, hilly properties that happen to abut. He gives a little finished syrup to the owners for the use of their trees. You'd never know where his orchard is. You take a major two-lane highway to Hancock, take a narrow two-way artery a couple miles to the village center, take a narrower one-lane paved road some miles up and over the hills, move onto a winding packed gravel road a mile or so, look hard for a minuscule open slot in the thick maples and oaks lining the road, and there it is, if you're good, only it's still down into the crowded woods a quarter mile.

———————————

How much do you collect in a season?

Well, it varies. Now last year I only made 50 percent. The year before that . . .

What do you mean 50 percent?

Well, 50 percent of my crop the year before. It can vary. Last year I made 50 gallons. The other year I made 100. You just don't know how it's going to go. This year I think it's warming up too fast. I think it's going to be short, you know. You don't get it now you're not going to get it. It's unusual to have this warm weather this early.

How long has a season gone that you can remember?

Oh, five years back I was sugaring here I couldn't even keep up with it. I was going right straight. Everybody around me wasn't doing a thing. Yeah, I was going straight. You see, this is kind of a northwest cast. A guy over there wasn't doing nothing, Byam wasn't doing nothing. Nobody around was making sugar, but I was going straight. I couldn't keep up with it! 'Course, I got a small outfit, you know.

So you really can't predict.

No, you take what Mother Nature gives you and that's it. You got to be adequate on your line, you got to check them. It takes me three or four hours to check these lines, walk them all out. And it's best to do it when the sap's running. So if there's a leak, you can see it, you can see it dripping. You just got to walk it right up on through. You got to be pretty accurate. The closer you keep track of them, the better they'll do for you.

Is there anything else you can do to urge the sap on beside clearing the brush out?

Well, it's just good management. You got good crowns on the trees. I just clean up the underbrush on them, let the sun in better. I come in on the weekend, work awhile, you know. The wood I cut down, if it's good for firewood, I use it.

I see pines there are starting to grow again. Going to have to cut them because they make shade.

When was the earliest date you remember that the sap started running?

Usually about Washington's Birthday, as a rule. I think one other year I made it before that, but very little. Last year I got started one little run in February but none enough to collect.

How late has it ever gone?

In April. If the snow is late, you can go into April.

Is it good to have the snow on the ground?

The snow is good because it keeps the roots wet. I've seen times you can go around with just your sneakers on and you can make just as much sugar, if the weather comes right. You can have stormy days with snow and rain and frosty nights. If it's warmer days, saps's going to run.

Can you tell out here by the flow and the trees what kind of grade you're going to get?

Not too well, no. I'm running only 2 percent this year. That's low. I like about 3, $3^1/_2$, but this year the sweetness of the sap is very low. I have a hydrometer. Last year I got up to 3, $3^1/_2$. It can vary. I was hoping it was going to change here.

The high percentage means you have less to boil away.

Right, you get up into the 3, $3^1/_2$, why, you're making a gallon of syrup with maybe 25, 30 gallons of sap. Right now I'm going 60, 65 gallons. The lower the content of the sugar the more it takes. You can't predict that. You take what Mother Nature gives. Nature has her own way of doing it.

You can use these tubes indefinitely?

Well, they're good for 20 years if you take care of them. When they get done, I wash them out right here on the line. I'll go to the high point and start water right on down through them, then come down to the spouts and flush them out right then and there. Take them down, roll them up, and put them into a dark room. A lot of guys will leave them out year-round. But if you get a lot of snow you have to dig them all out. I think it's just as easy to roll them up and take care of them.

I put them up in warm weather in November. They're about 4 feet up. You can keep them any height you want. Coming into my barrel you got to have them about right.

How long does it take to put up the lines?

It takes quite awhile. You don't put one of these up in a minute, you know. Especially if you're alone. You got to pull it a ways, you got to stretch it. You notice my lines are all stretched tight? Well, a lot of guys let them dangle, but I think you get better runs if everything is up there good and tight.

Is it just easier using the tubes as opposed to the buckets?

It's harder work doing the lines, but once you're set up it's just a matter of checking them. So it takes me a half hour to come in here and get what there is and I'm gone.

So it's more work at the beginning but less at the end.

Yeah, I put these lines up in good weather and no snow and I can walk pretty easy. I get a young fellow to help me. Steve Marchuk. Nice young fellow. Lives up above me. I kept him at the house there while he was building his. They're both nice kids.

Year-round Leo works keeping the firewood supply, the vegetable garden, the chickenhouse, and other chores at the nearby Harris Center, an enterprising foundation for conservation education. The tractor he uses to pick up the sap is from there. He drives the tractor with a platform hitched behind to the barrels at the trees. There he cranks on a pump that transfers the sap to other barrels on the platform. Then he drives the tractor back to the Harris Center barn where he transfers the sap from these barrels to a galvanized steel gathering tank on his pickup truck.

On the way we talk of the British tourist who was highly taken with this marvelous maple sugaring process he saw in New England one spring. So excited about the mercantile prospects of this process that the Britisher planned to return home and turn sugaring into a year-round operation. If only the maples would cooperate, we tell each other.

We drive the country road back to his sugarhouse behind his home. There his young neighbor, Steve Marchuk, helps him transfer the sap from the gathering tank to the storage tank perched high above the sugarhouse so that it can feed by gravity into the evaporator inside. Outside, Leo measures the sugar content of the sap. It's $2^1/_4$ percent.

Now how does the evaporator system work?

Well, right there where Steve is, that's where we start from. There's a storage tank up there on the roof, then the sap comes in here. This is the preheater here. Ten tubes in there 4 feet long. It comes out the bottom of it. That sweats it. See how it sweats as it's coming where it hits the heat. That takes the water out. That brings it in here at about 180, 190 degrees before it even hits the evaporator. So it saves you about 10, 12 percent of your time.

The evaporator has a whole series of pans in there, all divided out with the slot at the end, so that the sap goes where you want it to go. When this builds up steam, these tubes get awful hot. That pipe there vents the steam out. Then the sap comes out there. It's just beginning to sweeten, just beginning to tighten. It don't get really tight till it gets out here. The syrup is heavier than the sap so that sap keeps pushing the syrup ahead of it.

What temperature do you take it off at?

At 220. It's almost there now, just two more degrees. I usually go to 221.

How long does it take all the way through for a batch?

Depends on the sugar percentage. To make a gallon now it takes longer because it has a lower percentage. About an hour. At a higher percentage, at times you take it off every 20 minutes or so between. You're taking a small batch off.

What's a small batch?

Well, three quarts, four quarts. It's a small evaporator. It's only a 2 × 4 evaporator. The evaporator is only for 150 trees, not 400. So with a preheater and doing some extra time, you can get it done. It takes a little longer.

When you're drawing off, you open the fire door and throw some wood on so you don't burn your pans while you're drawing off. Keep the heat down—put more wood on top to hold it down. I did scorch it a couple times.

Steve Marchuk: How's the temperature?

You got three more degrees.

MAPLE SUGARING

What if you take it off three degrees below?

Well, you have light syrup, watered-down syrup. Here, I'll give you something that isn't watered down. [Pours syrup into a plastic shot glass.]

Look at that! Beautiful! That is really good! So what do you do after you draw off?

I strain it through the felt. I put it through two of them to get more of the dirt out, the sugar molasses out of it. It looks real black.

It's a continuous operation. You boil it as you get it.

You just boil it through. That's why I make such nice syrup like that, nice light syrup. You let it set and it starts to work. Then you start making dark syrup. The sooner you get it through, the lighter syrup you make. With this small rig I don't have no storage to speak of. I got to put it through.

Then when I get the finished syrup I put it in the pan there, put it on the burner, use that hydrometer, put it in that tank over there, and then bottle it.

You put it in gallons and what else?

Gallons, half-gallons, quarts, pints, whatever you think is going to go.

———————

Steve has been tending the fire and boiling off while Leo was out gathering sap. Inside the sugarhouse, the roaring fire, the heat, the steam, the rich marly aroma of maple all mix in a yearly ancient ritual. Every 15 minutes or so Steve goes to an adjoining room and hauls back more logs. He opens the firedoor and the blazing fire blasts out heat. He throws on some logs and slams the iron door with a clank. Then he and Leo keep a watchful eye on the energetic boiling sap in the evaporator. If the sap boils too much and threatens to overflow, they cut down the heat.

Last year Leo sold all his syrup except for one gallon. The quality doesn't change over a year, although possibly a plastic taste from the jug may begin to surface. For that gallon he'll run it through the evaporator again to freshen it up.

If maple syrup is left at room temperature and opened, it may grow some mold. All you have to do, Leo says, is reheat it, skim it, put it back, and it's as good as ever. Some people put it in the refrigerator once the seal is broken. You can put syrup in a freezer. "If it's good syrup," he says, "it won't freeze."

How much wood does it take for a season?

Oh, it takes me about ten cords. I'm going through wood like crazy for what little I made. I gone through two full tiers there already. I ain't made that much, I don't know, a dozen, 15 gallons I guess. But you make tremendously nice syrup when you're on a low sugar content. You get on a higher content, you go dark quicker. You want a little more?

Oh, no, I can't drink all your profits. Well, just a little. I love this stuff.

Steve: What is it? Boil sap three weeks of the year, cut wood the rest of the year!

I suppose you'd like oak and maple to burn.

I usually like hard wood. Makes a better fire, you don't have to keep after it all the time. Pine, you just have to chase it all the time.

No, it's not easy. It's all work, that's for sure. 'Course, the sugarhouse isn't quite big enough. Well, 220 is usually good syrup. Down here in the valley most of the time I go 221. Different altitude.

MAPLE SUGARING

How late do you stay out here?

Well, last night it was midnight before I got out of here. Probably midnight again tonight.

Steve: You better go to sleep before that. I know I'm going to work tomorrow so I can rest!

I think I'm going to. I'm up at three o'clock. It makes a long day. I'm out here pushing this. It's nothing to put 16 hours here. I'm fortunate to get Steve here so I can go up and get it and keep it going.

Here, look at the stuff in the felt. See the stuff that's catching. A lot of these guys, they don't strain, strain once maybe and that's it. You open a jug and you get that much black molasses stuff on the bottom.

Steve: That's how they get 14-pound gallons.

Do you have people who buy from you every year?

Oh, yeah. I don't advertise too much. It's word of mouth. Mostly it's sold here. It's really funny. You get one, then bang, you get three sales right off. Then it levels off for awhile. Then you get one and sure as the devil you get two or three more behind it.

Do you usually sell all you make?

Yeah, as I say I usually can make 50 to 100 gallons.

This little shack was given me. I put wood into it awhile. Then I got the urge to sugaring so I made it into a sugarhouse. It's just a small sugarhouse, ain't much to it. You know, you're only in here about five or six weeks in spring. During the summer it gets junked up. When I start sugaring, the house gets junked up. I got to take it all out!

The bigger operations do it differently, I suppose.

They have all these new inventions that cut the sap to about

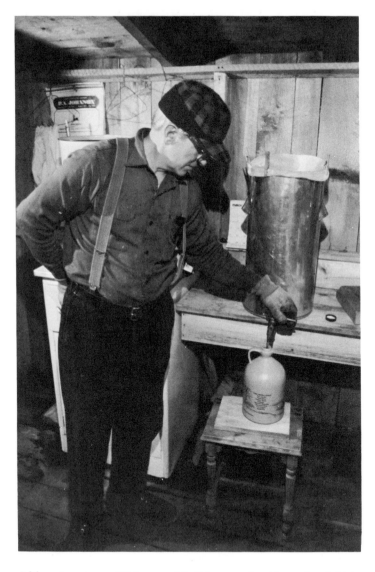

I like mine nice and light. . . . It's light syrup but it's good and thick. . . . It almost sticks to your teeth.

MAPLE SUGARING

7 or 8 percent before it gets in there. Then it doesn't take you long to boil it. It's a big investment, 10,000-dollar investment.

That takes the water right out of it. Brings it up to sweet sap, real sweet, almost syrup. Bascom over there in Alstead—what'd he say?—they were making 45 gallons a minute. 'Course, they're a big outfit. They tap about 30,000, 40,000 trees.

What do you personally look for in a good syrup?

I like mine nice and light. I make it heavy, that's what a lot of them don't. It's light syrup but it's good and thick. A lot of them make it almost like water.
Steve: But does it stay on the old cakes?
Yeah. It's thick, but it's light, transparent. It almost sticks to your teeth. A lot of guys just run it straight on through, you know. They don't filter it too much.

How do you make a thicker syrup?

By going to the 221, I know I'm making a heavy syrup. You go to 218 you got a much lighter syrup. See what I mean? That's where a lot of them are doing it at. It's a short year and they're cutting their weight down. They're making more doing it that way, putting up more volume. Two or three points less, you gain quite a bit [of volume]. It takes an extra half hour to get it up to 220, so you're losing quite a bit. But I wouldn't do it any other way anyway.

Then if you got syrup that don't keep, it hasn't been cooked enough. It can sour, you know, if it ain't cooked hot enough. At 216 or 217 it ain't going to keep good. It'll be sweet on pancakes, but it'll go right straight through them. That sort of thing.

How much do you use in a season?

We don't use very much. I taste quite a bit. I'm not supposed to have too many sweets now. I do have pancakes once in awhile. I really like to smother them!

EMMA BAILEY

Auctioneering

Emma Bailey

Brattleboro, Vermont

One of the delights of a New England summer is to spend an afternoon in a big old barn or under a green and white auction tent. The atmosphere is friendly and eager and, if some prized items are up for bid, electric. A major part of that atmosphere is the auctioneer. These had always been men—that is, until Emma Bailey came along.

At 74 Emma is intelligent, beautiful, articulate, clear, precise, sharp, and aware. Perfect for an auctioneer.

She's retired now, but in her comfortable homey living room we talk of her active years in auctioneering, from 1952 to the early 1970s, when auctions were more cheery and accessible than most are today. Emma was the first woman to belong to the National Auctioneering Association, in a way, the first woman to break the sex barrier. However, she's less interested in that than in the changes that have happened in auctioneering over the years, the large-scale social factors that have influenced the direction and tone of auctions, and how auctions fit into her life and the lives of other New Englanders. Not only is she the family historian (her husband's Yankee side goes back to the 1600s), but she loves all history.

Her book, *Sold to the Lady in the Green Hat; America's First Woman Auctioneer*, was published by Dodd, Mead in 1962. It tells of her auctioneering life in her barn in Brattleboro during the years when her reputation grew to a national level. The book is on a nearby shelf in a room of many lovingly framed pictures of her family and friends. She sits in a red chair and wears a blue skirt and an attractive white blouse with blue trim on the collar. She's talked enough to others about being the first woman this and that. She'd rather talk about the bigger picture of auctions. She'd rather have others understand

and enjoy what she understands and enjoys—the good ol' New England auction.

———————————

I have to ask you what the first spark was that got you interested in auctioneering. How did it all begin?

I have a very dim recollection of an auction when my family lived in New Jersey. I must have been in the third grade. I remember feeling so badly because all the furniture was outdoors. In those days, the auctions were sheriff's sales. I never saw or heard of one again until I read *The Mayor of Casterbridge*, when he auctioned off his wife. The negative aspect continued.

Then when I got older, what changed my negative aspect was my tremendous interest in American history. Part of it was due to my husband's grandmother from Danbury, Connecticut (they're quick to tell you that Connecticut settled Vermont!). They had up in the attic a beautiful, old, old cradle and I remember being fascinated by the workmanship. So then my interest began to combine history with workmanship.

Also, one of my husband's ancestors married into the Goddard family that made the Goddard furniture. That made it more interesting. Then we came to Vermont in 1944. I became terribly interested in going to the local auctions because my friends would say We just pack a picnic and go to the auctions like a fair. So I began to do that. That's how it grew.

During the war the sheriff's idea of an auction became less prominent. It was the scarcity that gave auctions an elitism, a scarcity of items, and at that time everybody wanted new things. Previous to that, because everybody liked what was new, they didn't separate value from what they had. So the young people, from lack of funds and scarcity of materials, which the war produced, became very interested in buying usable, sturdy chests of drawers. They weren't as antique-conscious as they were of usable goods; they were more family-conscious.

AUCTIONEERING

So they were more interested in the practical value than in a so-called inherent value of these pieces.

Right. I became disturbed at this, so much so that to my own disadvantage I'd say, Well, I don't think you'd want to sell that, you should save that. And to this day, I meet someone sometimes who says, You know, Emma, I'm so glad you didn't have me sell that piece, I saw one just like it in the museum lately or in a magazine. But you see, most auctioneers don't do that. Now, most auctioneers will say, once called in, Everything I see is to be here when I sell. Sometimes I'd say to the seller, Well, you have children and grandchildren, you should keep that.

At what point did you become an auctioneer? What made you decide?

The children were growing up fast, inflation was setting in quicker than the children were growing up, it seemed, and it just seemed that it might be good to have some extra money coming in. But in the meantime, I didn't want to be away from home five days a week. I was doing some substitute teaching, but I wanted something that would use the property that we had bought, and being very family-oriented, something that would include the whole family.

There must have been something that urged you on, that made you say, all right, I'm going to be an auctioneer.

One time I was at an auction and this auctioneer was just stumbling all over himself. Now this *actually* happened. He got so excited, he got stuttering so badly, that his false teeth flew out! And I thought to myself, good grief, I could do better than that. Unfortunately, he was an old Yankee and there was a group of Yankees who heckled him to death.

Well, anyway, I have to be very interested in anything I do. I couldn't work in a factory and do the same thing every day.

So in a sense auctioneering presented itself to you.

Yes, it presented itself to fill my need. And I had absolutely no thoughts about women's lib. Because I'm not that type of person.

But as soon as you decided to go into auctioneering, it must have hit you that this is not normally done by a woman.

I don't think so. I'm apt to act. When this dear man lost his teeth and I was thinking, goodness, I could do as well as he is or better, the woman next to me said, Emma, you could do better than he, and I said, Yes, I think I could. Well, you ought to give it some thought, she said jokingly. She planted the whole seed. I tried to discuss it with my family and they were automatically against it. My husband's famous words were, "If there were to be women auctioneers in Vermont, they wouldn't have waited for you." That's a good quote because he's a typical Yankee. He's not an antifeminist; it's just that you do your chores and I'll do mine.

I felt badly about this poor man's confusion. These hecklers didn't mean it unkindly. They were there at every auction; they were people he knew well, but they made life miserable for him. That was real Yankee humor, you know. To heckle people is their sense of humor.

So I thought about it and went to the library and got out books. But there were no books on auctioneers per se at that time. In fact, somebody said once, a little unkindly, It's you and your book that got the prices so high and got everybody interested. Nobody cared before that, which is true.

Auctions were different then.

People would come to auctions because it was a neighborhood thing. They would like something either from Aunt Helen's or Aunt Mary's or their neighbor's house as a memento. Then with the scarcity of the war, they were interested in buying things.

How did you generate interest in your auctions? What were some things you did?

It always amused people. Spontaneously, I could always see something useful about that item other than what it was designed to be. Sometimes I'd say, You know, this would make a perfect room divider, perfect for the baby's room. That was the period of the commodes, the washstands, that sold for 50 cents, rarely over a dollar. Sometimes I'd say, Well, now why don't you take one of these commodes and turn it into a baby's dressing table! Put a pad on the top and have places to keep the diapers. Pretty soon people'd come and say, Do you have one of those baby's dressing tables? "Oh, you mean a commode!"

Was there a certain length of time that you as a woman had to have before being accepted in the auctioneering world?

No, I was immediately accepted. But I did have a basic problem. The man who lost his teeth knew through word of mouth that I had applied for a license, but he also knew that he could do nothing to stop me until there was an actual ad in the paper. When we printed our first ad sale, he went to the zoning board. I was stopped by the zoning board two days before the actual auction was scheduled.

Now that turned out to be a good thing. The fact that I was stopped gave me publicity that I needed.

There's nothing like censorship in one form or another to stir interest.

Exactly, you used the right word.

How long did it take you to get your first auction going?

About three weeks later. Now, of course, everybody was interested and wanting to watch this strange woman. They came from Greenfield and Keene, everywhere our fliers went, to watch this strange woman perform.

Her family hay barn on Black Mountain Road was converted to an auction barn. She couldn't then buy and resell items so she operated on a straight commission of 25 percent; she provided the place, advertising, and arranging. Some auctioneers got less if the sellers supplied workers and expenses.

She learned a few lessons fast. A knowledgeable friend gave her some words of wisdom about a notorious colleague. He warned her to never let the man get anywhere near the money box. One time when she was about to start an auction, he came up to her and said, "Mrs. Bailey, I brought over three of my sons to help you and their aprons are all set up with change." He said each apron had $100 worth of change. Emma said, "Thank you for the offer, but, no, thank you." The man wouldn't have had $100 in the aprons, but he would have deducted $100 each apron for himself afterward.

Once she had a large antique collection advertised in *The New York Times* and another well-known colleague saw the ad. Over the years he came up to her auctions several times. After Emma was in the business for five or six years, he invited her to join the association.

Did membership in the association help you in any way?

No. Actually, it became a burden, because every woman in the United States who was connected with auctions or had always wanted to be an auctioneer wrote me. One woman said, "My father was an auctioneer, my grandfather, my brothers, but they would never let me get up on the block, and I know I could have done better than they lots of times."

But within that first year of my being a member, they must have had about 24 women, with a steady increase—now high in the hundreds. But they never gave me any credit. The women in the eastern part of the United States did not pick it up like the women in the Middle West did. A friend told me that in the Middle West that was about the only way they sold.

Why was it so unusual, if not totally impossible, for a woman to get on the block?

I really think it had been something only men did.

It's not as if they're chopping down oak trees with hand axes or something.

No. And I also think it was the sheriff attitudes, because in New England the auctions were mainly for settlement of debts.

What was the most prized item you sold?

Now you must remember I'm an historian. So size and price don't mean as much to me as they might to other people. One of the prize items can be seen in the Shelburne Museum on Lake Champlain in Vermont; to me it is a marvelous example of early carving in American history. It's a left-hand clothes stick. The handle went right up to where your elbow would stop—but *beautifully* carved! The fingers were worn raw from lifting heavy things. A complete wrist and a shapely arm.

In my imagination, that was carved by a groom for his bride. He wanted her to have more than a forked stick. Now I sold it to a dealer. A dealer sold it to another dealer. A third dealer sold it to Mrs. Webb, who originated the Shelburne Museum. The last time I was up there it was on exhibit in the Vermont House. Absolutely beautiful. It was bleached white from years of homemade soap. Now this person was left-handed, which also made it different. Maybe they could have bought one from the traveling peddler, but that would have been right-handed. It was *left*-handed.

It was custom-made.

Oh, no, no, not custom-made. Made by someone who *loved* her! She could have used a forked stick. Everybody used a forked stick. Why was this one special?

Because she was special.

Because she was special.

The thing that I find a little disturbing is that people want an exact copy of what is in *Antiques Magazine*. But when you get to Vermont furniture you must be a little bit flexible because the Vermont craftsman did things the way he wanted them. His client would go and say, I want a highboy but I want it to fit in *this* space. Imagine people coming to an auction with a tape measure to measure a highboy. If it isn't such and such many inches, it's not authentic.

She wants it to fit *that* space, and she wants it part bird's-eye maple and part cherry. So he builds it to her specifications. Some independent Yankee wants a highboy made that way to fit a certain space for a certain reason.

You must also remember with antique furniture that the people who worked for Mr. Goddard and any of the other well-known early furniture makers, when they made furniture for their own daughters and their own wives and their own families, they put in their own little creative twists. They followed Mr. Goddard all week long. But some people will come with the book under their arm and what they're looking for must be exactly like it, and those are generally one of a kind. But that to me is the most interesting part of the bunch.

The unique pieces.

The unusual. As long as it's the period and as long as it's the woods, you have a find. For instance, we had some early, early Bennington ware that was never signed. The very earliest Bennington made by Norton and the others were never signed. He got through with the Revolutionary War and he remembered how beautiful the clay was up here. He came back from Connecticut and started his clay factory. Some were just *beautiful*. There was one woman who was so upset that they weren't signed that she wouldn't bid on them, poor soul. If she had gone over to the Bennington Museum she would have known what was passing by. But the dealers, they knew what was happening.

What were some of the changes during your active years?

The changes during those years were the changes during the last half of those years. It was inflationary. At the end of the war, scarcity continued for quite some time with an increased appreciation. More and more was being written and the antique interest was becoming greater. The war had a lot to do with the increase in prices, too, because sheriff sales were no longer used. And particularly Brattleboro with our lovely big houses with sheds and barns where everything was stored. During the war there was a housing scarcity; they were being converted into apartments and therefore we had the barns to clean out and the attics to clean out. Vermonters are squirrels, everything would get squirreled away under the eaves. All this came out from under the eaves. And when people kept seeing what money was coming out of the eaves, elderly people would decide to sell and go into an apartment.

In a similar thought, if you had a piece that you sold at a given price in your active days and the same piece today, would it be the same price, given inflation?

Not always. You must keep in consideration that some things are faddish. Some things are extremely popular for awhile; they go to the top of what the traffic will bear and then people lose interest because the price is so high. Then the interest falls to the next in line. Highboys, lowboys, those have gone out of sight. People who have them find it equally profitable to give it to a museum, get a good evaluation, take it off their income tax, and the piece lives on forever with their name on it. And other things keep moving up. What has happened is that things become older faster.

You also have to take into consideration that furniture companies immediately start reproducing. When that happens, interest drops because people are always worried. We had a beautiful collection of genuine milk glass blown at the end of the period. The dealers wouldn't touch it. They knew it was genuine, I knew it was genuine, but there was so much of it in Woolworth's, so much of it given away with coupons, that doubt set in.

That could kill an auction.

It does. We had competitiveness between dealers. But what happens now is a little unfair to the seller. Remember that every auctioneer has to make the seller feel that he's got the highest possible price and the buyer feel he's got a prize at the lowest possible price. That requires skill.

———

When Emma says that items today are getting older faster, she means that there was a time when antiques were at least 75 years

Remember that every auctioneer has to make the seller feel that he's got the highest possible price and the buyer feel he's got a prize at the lowest possible price. That requires skill.

old before they could be called "antiques." Now things that people considered junk when she was auctioneering not so long ago are being called antiques. It almost seems that if people don't remember something from their own experience, it's therefore an antique.

In her day, competition between auctioneers was keen, and this was an advantage, especially to the seller. Today some dealers form a consortium almost. One auctioneer, Emma points out, will say, Now I'm interested in those Windsor chairs. The other man says, All right, I'll lay off those, but I want that Pembroke table. "Yeah, but I want that cut-glass punch bowl." On it goes.

"The seller is being gypped," she says. "The seller is not getting top price. You need competition."

Even now Emma gets letters in spring from those people remembering fondly their time at her auction barn and how as kids they enjoyed the afternoon playing under apple trees while mother and father were bidding inside. They write to say that they want their children to have the same wonderful time. But Emma has to say that "time stops with memories" and that those good times have stopped.

You mentioned the skill it takes to please both sides and to go down the middle very judiciously. What is that skill? What does that entail?

The skill is for the auctioneer to know exactly every plus of that piece. Some of them don't because they're so busy selling that they don't have time for research. The auctioneer should take time to listen to the seller tell about these family pieces. Because they're revealing a lot of history. Now some auctioneers will go right in, they start listing, they get so involved that they don't *listen*. Again, you have a woman's feeling of listening to the history. Do your research. Then you draw out every important bit about that particular item—the woods, the period, the family history, its possibilities, its probabilities.

And you keep reminding them that you won't find this same item on every maple tree in Vermont. Some people get the impression that Vermont is chock-full of everything they want, and if they don't get it at this auction, they'll get it at next week's auction. It just isn't so.

Are there certain skills you developed in assessing your crowd?

Oh, yes, you can assess them in one glance. You always know the dealers because they stand aloof and untouchable. Because they don't want to be caught looking at anything. And in one glance, they know what they want, just one quick glance.

You can also pick out the troublemakers. For instance, this one man—and there's one at *every* auction—always considers himself an authority on everything. And you can tell them, too. One man would go around and turn over chairs and to these innocent old ladies he'd say, They aren't very good, aren't turned right, it isn't the right wood. It's to discourage anyone else, you see.

What are some suggestions you have for ordinary people about attending auctions?

That depends on the ads. Thursday night is advertisement night in the summer months. Now the bullet lines are your antiques. Then you go on from your antiques to your Almost Old. Then the Not So Old.

Is this standard?

Well, mine wasn't standard. Some things that I created have become standard, through other people picking them up and using them. I would go Antique, Almost Antique, On the Way to Being Antique, You Wouldn't Dare Call It Antique!

We got a letter from a woman who used to have a summer place here in Brattleboro. She said, I don't come to Vermont very often, but your auctions were the best. After we became accustomed to yours, we couldn't stand anybody else. Yours were the best. My prized piece today is when you picked up an old silver vase all dark and discolored and you just worked on me to have it. Well, I knew she was a woman of good taste and I just said, Now Mrs. North, this would be perfect in your house. Finally she bought it. When I got home, I polished it and cleaned it, she said. The shocking thing were the initials EBH on it— those were my grandfather's initials, she said. His name was Hoyt. The piece was made in Connecticut. I wrote back and said, When you get ready to send it to Believe It or Not, add another sentence. My husband's grandparent on his maternal side was E. B. Hoyt from Danbury. I think you're going to find out that we're related!

Isn't that something? What if a novice went to an auction out of curiosity and for something he needed? What would be some of the things he should know?

Now, you said two important words. If he's there for curiosity, it's one thing. If he's there for a need, that's another. If he bids for a need, he may go a little bit further than what it's worth; for him it fulfills a need. If it's an item for curiosity, it depends what field his curiosity is.

The old Sandwich glassmakers at the end of the day, if there was liquid glass left over, could make whatever they wanted for themselves. Some of them would do something just a wee bit different. For years one such Sandwich glass worker did that and when his daughter died there was a huge closet full of all these things he did. Now what if you get a woman like the Bennington woman, she wants the name Bennington on it, and this man didn't sign them? Those pieces are more valuable. Because of the wonderful Vermont artisans who did things their way.

If ordinary people at an auction can spot the dealer, is that something to pay attention to?

If they really want it bad enough, the people stay in it because the dealer has to make a profit, where the others don't need to.

What would you say to people who wanted to be auctioneers, given your wonderful background and what you've seen through your active years?

Well, they've got to like people first. The hardest thing in the world is to deal with people, and if they don't like people, forget it. They've got to study. Everybody who goes into the business seems to think they're going to have nothing but antiques because that's where the money is. They must be prepared for a great change in the people. The people are most knowledgeable today. The library shelves are full of books on antiques now.

Be prepared that a successful auction, unless it's at Sotheby's in New York, has to be a mixture of everything to suit the general public. Now from the seller's point of view, I always explain before an auction, you want a certain price on this, but you're going to forget all the *junk* that we're going to sell out of the barn and out of the cellar, stuff in the attic that you wouldn't even want to dust off. Now you remember that balance for these two pieces. When these two pieces don't get exactly what you want, remember what you're getting for junk!

Do you know fairly accurately the price you're going to get for a particular item?

I have an aim. But I'm also flexible for the people. After the war when things were scarce and hard, this young girl came to one of our auctions with her two children. It was a local auction, she was a local girl. The kind of auctions I like best. We all knew that she was a young widow and her husband did not come back from the war. We all knew that. And we all knew that she was a thoughtful, gentle mother and wanted the best for her two children. A treadle sewing machine came up. Well, those who didn't know it never had a chance. That girl took that treadle sewing machine home. Those who knew it kept still. There was a silence. They kept still.

How nice. How did you arrange that?

The first bid was the only thing I saw. And I'm sure God will forgive me, and I don't care if I burn in hell for that. That girl needed that sewing machine. That is the Vermont auction. It's neighbor for neighbor. And if you make more money than you expected, fine. Lots of people now won't go to auctions anymore because they feel it's no longer neighbor for neighbor. They too much favor the dealer.

That's a change you don't favor.

Well, I can't say that because an auction without a dealer is of no interest, but know your people, know your clientele. That girl needed a sewing machine. I knew she needed it, people around her knew she needed it. If I had let that sewing machine go up to maybe 15 dollars that day, all the local people would have *hated* me. And I'm a person who puts relationships before money, and that is why I'm not rich today. But I can walk downtown and visit with my neighbors.

DAVE FOSTER

Boatbuilding

Dave Foster

Rockport, Maine

On a warm, breezy, *perfect* Maine shore day, we settle under a friendly tree with the full breadth of the blue and rocky Rockport harbor in front of us. All shapes of sailboats and work boats are anchored in the inlet, some of them built by hand in the nearby Apprenticeshop, a boatbuilding school.

This school is one of a growing number that share the same ideals: to get back to wooden boats, to make boats by hand, and to think in terms of beauty as well as utility. The art was on its way out of hand-me-down existence during the 1950s and '60s when fiberglass inundated the boat world. Boatbuilders like Dave Foster were on the way out, too, and with them some of the ancient treasured knowledge that can only pass on directly through apprentices.

Dave has built boats since he was 17. He owned a shop on Cape Cod, and then through the decades worked at different boatyards until ten years ago. At that time, he heard about the resurrecting work of the Apprenticeshop and joined it as a teacher, a passer-along of hand-and-wood work that only a master can offer.

Maine is a good setting. Its tradition of boatbuilding is long and full of pride. Many fishermen made their own boats in the old days and their art reached heights that Dave hated to see disappear. All sorts of boats are made, big and small, sailing and rowing. Some of the historic boats have fanciful names, too. Penobscot Bay Pinky. Delaware Ducker. Susan Skiff. Lighthouse Pea Pod. Five Islands Boat. Prospect Marsh Pinky. Norwegian Holmsbu Pram. Hurricane Island Pulling Boat.

Dave talks about what makes a good boat, how the 5,000-year-old art is regaining life today, and why the priorities of good boatbuilding reflect some of the older values that younger men and women are incorporating into their lives.

You build historic boats mostly, is that right?

Yes, work boats. People use them today as recreational boats. Right out there is a Newfound skiff about 17 feet. The one up ahead of it is a New Jersey melon seed. The Newfound boat was used for sealing. The melon seed was a hunting boat, duck hunting. We got much of our information about how boats should be built often times from the Smithsonian Institute. All these plans for historic boats pretty much originate from a guy named Howard Chapelle in the thirties. During the Depression on a grant, he took the lines of boats that were derelicts in New England and around the country and recorded them in four or five books. If that hadn't happened, this would have been lost.

That was a stroke of luck. How far back are the designs traced?

A lot from the early 1800s, 1850s.

What kind of woods are the best?

Almost all the boats built in New England have oak, preferably white oak, for the basic structure of the boat, what they call the backbone, the keel, and the frame. It's like a house frame. A boat also has a frame structure and all the structural members normally would be white oak. And white oak can be steam-bent very nicely. You steam it and bend it to many shapes, so it's ideally suited for boats.

For planking, when you get into building yachts, you talk more about exotic types of wood like Honduras mahogany and teak. Teak is nice because you don't have to paint it. Just leave it natural and soon it turns gray. Mahogany and those kinds of woods are expensive and nice to look at, but they don't necessarily last any longer. The type of boats we build in Maine—the work boats—we try to build those out of the original woods they were built out of, all native woods.

There must have been a great expertise in boatbuilding in New England because of the fishing and whaling industries. Has this knowledge dissipated much?

Oh, yes, but it's coming back now. It's part of the whole search for satisfying work to do. People we have here at the shop learning to build boats are much more highly educated than the people who were learning boatbuilding 40 or 50 years ago. Most of these people today have graduated from college, some have master's degrees. It's part of going back to using their hands, part of a more satisfying way of life.

I graduated from high school in the mid-forties and people then thought about how much money they could make doing this or that. And, of course, boatbuilding was not one of those things. You had to be a little crazy wanting to do that. It's always been a not very high-paying thing. You have to have a lot of skill and a lot of tools. Even carpenters can have less skill and just a few tools and make as much or more money than a boatbuilder. So it's never been high-paying, but it has a certain element of romanticism!

Do you think that people who build boats today with such care build boats as well as they used to in the 1800s?

Oh, undoubtedly. I think the emphasis is different now. I think that people always had pride in their work, but the boats then were much more expendable because the boats were only a means to an end. Like these dories out there with the nets. All the fishermen care about is that the dory stays afloat to keep the net in. He's not particularly interested in any other aspect of the boat, just that it floats and it lasts. So they didn't pay attention to the little details and they certainly didn't think in terms of the boat lasting 50 years. And they didn't have the materials that we have now. They used mostly wrought iron in the early 1800s. They knew that the iron was going to rust away, nails and screws. The boat would be pretty much up to rebuilding after 30 years or so.

Today with bronze and stainless steel and all these nonferrous alloys, and if it's good wood and taken care of, it can last for an incredible amount of time. Today people are sometimes perfectionists about everything. The standards that they set for themselves are much higher than the boat really demands. It's the difference between making a fine piece of furniture that's going to be protected and a boat that's going to be out in the elements. The boat is somewhere in between. Some of the fittings have to be good, but the boat isn't going to be a piece of furniture for very long. That's a great disappointment for some people when they spend a lot of time on a boat and they begin to lose sight of what the boat really is. It's a way to get around on the water, and it's going to get scratched.

In a sense, you're almost saying that, through this change of values, a renaissance of values almost, you're taking the historic boats and actually improving them.

They can't be improved on very much in terms of shape, but they can be improved on in some minor ways. Like today we have waterproof glue. We can put together two pieces of wood. If you need a piece of wood 16 feet long and you can't get a perfect piece, you can scarf two pieces together, what we call plank scarf. Whereas in the old days if you were limited to 16-foot planks, you had to use whatever you had. We have some rubber-type compounds that stay much more elastic, but they had nothing like that.

Are the tools different, too?

Hand tools are pretty much the same. In fact, people who build boats prefer old tools. It's not only that old tools are less money. They'll haunt flea markets and secondhand stores looking for old tools and they seem to think they're better. Another thing is that a lot of tools have been discontinued. Now we have a limited variety of tools, but they're beginning to come back.

Do you yourself find them better?

I really don't think they have better steeling. Some do, but the design is usually a little bit nicer. They tend to make things a little bit more awkward now for hand tools. There's a big interest in woodworking in this country and now there's a big demand for

64

specialty tool shops. A few years ago your whole selection of tools had to come from the local hardware store. Now there's so much information, books and magazines; it's one of the advantages for people wanting to learn boatbuilding.

Do you think that such interest in tools and fine boatbuilding carries over into other aspects of life?

Oh, definitely with these people. For most of them, if they were to build a house, it wouldn't be just an ordinary house. They tend to lean toward post-and-beam construction, something that shows a lot of craftsmanship. They're not going to build just an FHA house with vinyl siding. A lot of them would be the type who would like to find a 1948 pickup truck or a Ford wooden stationwagon. It doesn't seem to matter if it's going to take more work to maintain or run. The same people are 90 percent ecology-minded.

That's a departure, don't you think, from the people who built these boat designs originally?

Oh, yes, definitely. That was really the discouraging thing about it when I started in boatyards. I actually gave up boatbuilding about 1970 for a couple years because it was impossible to get anyone . . . well, a boatyard today still can't afford to pay and teach someone all this stuff about boatbuilding while the customer is paying the bill. That doesn't work. That's why these boatbuilding schools became necessary. The old system before minimum wage, you could go to a boatyard and they'd pay you hardly anything, but you could survive on it and they had time to teach you. That's the way I learned it. They'd take time because they knew they weren't paying you a lot of money.

———————

During Dave's early boatbuilding days, the information about the art was extremely limited. He remembers a couple of books, but they were designed for the backyard boatbuilder and assumed too much; no detailed explanations of the process a builder had to go through was given. The books, he says, have improved vastly over the years.

The only boat he has now of all that he built is a canoe. The others were for customers; some of them were big two-masters with large cabins for long-distance sailing. He sold the boats but kept the skills.

In the school he supervises and teaches 14 students (currently, one woman). Normally, one boat is assigned to every two builders. This winter eight boats are being built. Some are as big as a whale, others as lithe and handsome as a dolphin.

———————

What kind of skills does it take innately for boatbuilding? What eventually do you develop?

At the beginning we have a lot of people who have no skills. They haven't tried even any woodwork. Most people can develop the basic woodworking skills. But what you're *really* developing in boatbuilding is that you have to train your eye. Most of us are used to dealing with everything in straight lines. The people may have made some bookcases or built a garage. When you get into building boats where everything is curves, there's such a thing as what we call a fair curve which is pleasing to the eye. It can be a changing curve, but it doesn't have anything in it that the eye is going to notice that right here is where it takes a change. It's going to be a gradual flowing curve.

It takes some good skill to produce that.

Yes, it's not a cut-and-dry thing where you measure everything. You have to sight things, you have to look at things, especially on traditional boats. The shape of the boat may be well defined, but sometimes the construction hasn't been well recorded accurately. The sizing and proportions are a matter of aesthetics. A lot of that has traditionally been left up to the boatbuilder. So a person has to develop a feel for what looks right, what would look too big, what kind of a cleat would look too big on that wood, what would be strong enough. There's a retraining of yourself to think

Most of us are used to dealing with everything in straight lines. . . . When you get into building boats where everything is curves, there is such a thing as what we call a fair curve which is pleasing to the eye.

about, say, if you're planing pine, you have to also sight along the edge of it to see that it looks right.

So you have to bring a lot of aesthetics to boatbuilding, a sense of what is pleasing and beautiful to look at.

Yes. People who don't have that building a boat in their backyards, it usually stands out from a boat built by a boatbuilder.

DAVE FOSTER

The little details are not quite right. It's not that they're off a whole lot, but they're off just enough.

I imagine you can see that yourself easily.

You can notice it. If there were two professional boatbuilders up here, one would be favored because he could make things look just right. Particularly in Maine. A lot of boats in Maine were built entirely by eye. The builders made a little half-model, which they carved out. Lobster boatbuilders still do it. They carve out a model. Often it's an evolution. They go with one for two years but if they didn't quite like the way it went through the water they changed it a little. The model is just giving them the shape of the boat. They work from the model and build the boat. A lot of it is done just by eye. Their eye is so developed that they can see just the slightest thing that doesn't look right as they're building it.

What relationship does the fair curve have to do with the utilitarian part of a boat. Is there any relationship?

A slight one. If the boat doesn't have a fair smooth curve through the water it's going to meet more resistance, but it's pretty negligible. It's mostly a matter of aesthetics and appearance. Of course, wood tends to bend that way anyway. Wood *wants* to bend a nice curve. So that's all part of the process.

The thing that people find most amazing when they start to build boats is what you can do with wood when you steam it. You can take this piece of oak that's pretty rigid, say it's 2 inches by 2 inches, steam it a couple hours and with a little push and pull you can bend it all around.

A boat seems too complex. I can remember that it seemed impossible that you could build something like that. Taken one step at a time and you know how to do it, there isn't any mystery to it. Each step is fairly simple.

How long does it take to build a boat?

A person just beginning takes much longer than someone who knows how to do it. An experienced boatbuilder can build ten of

It's mostly a matter of aesthetics and appearance. Of course, wood tends to bend that way anyway. Wood wants to bend a nice curve.

these little boats in a year, like that melon seed. A beginner may take all year, or six or eight months with two people. They have to think about every step, but after you've been doing it a while it becomes automatic. When I'm building a boat, they can't understand how I'm doing it so easily and so quickly. They're looking to see what I *haven't* done right. It looks too easy. But when you know how to do something, there's no wasted motion.

How many pieces of wood does a boat like that melon seed have?

Oh, endless, it seems. It must have 20 planks, 40 frames—I'd say over 150 pieces. We don't cut our wood from a tree, but it's the next best thing. It's just a tree slabbed off with bark on the edges. We need a lot of curved pieces. None of the planks on a boat are straight, they're all shaped.

During the low point of boatbuilding about 25 years ago, businesses that specialized in boat lumber went into another line. Dave remembers one of the places he got lumber in Charlestown, Massachusetts. Now the yard sells Formica, plywood, and cabinet hardware. "Nobody would ever know it was a boat lumberyard," he says.

The same thing happened with marine hardware. In those bleak fiberglass days, a serious boatbuilder could hardly find any business that sold anything else but stainless-steel hardware, which is totally inappropriate for traditional boats.

Certain nails are used a lot to join planks together on boats. Ten years ago it was almost impossible to find any in this country. Boatbuilders had to fasten their boats with rivets that they got from Norway. Fortunately, with the recent surge of interest, some companies in the United States now manufacture boat nails and other marine hardware. It's even easier now to get specialized boat lumber.

A wooden boat has so much lustre and beauty to it, but what are some of the disadvantages to a wooden boat?

A lot of people today just want to get out in their boat during the boating seasons. They don't want to think about it the rest of the year. That's not a real boat person. That's just someone who's thinking of another form of recreation. The boat is just an object to get him out waterskiing or whatever. A wood boat takes a lot more maintenance. There's painting, which is done almost on a yearly basis, sanding and painting. A well-built and well-maintained wooden boat doesn't require a lot of work. The fiberglass boat was presented as a boat that didn't need any maintenance. People get one and they find out they still have to paint the bottom or paint the topside and wax them yearly. But whatever you might say, in the end there's less maintenance on a fiberglass boat. You usually have an aluminum mast and you don't have to do anything with that.

The boating public is divided into two camps. The wooden boat people look down their noses at the fiberglass boats, and the fiberglass people say, Well, let them go ahead, we can be out sailing while they're still working on their boats. I think that people with an all-wooden boat enjoy working on it. That's part of the whole thing. When I was growing up, the boatyard was like a club. Everybody was working on their boats. You don't see that today. The boatyards are all so expensive. They mostly don't let people do much work on their boats, and so it's very formal.

It's really changed.

Oh, yes. The old-time boatyard, which was sort of a boating club, a sailing club, people were there all the time.

HUGH TUTTLE

Family Farming

Hugh Tuttle

Dover Point, New Hampshire

The Tuttle farm is the oldest direct-line family farm in the United States. The title and tilling of the land have passed from father to son since the original John Tuttle obtained the land grant in 1632. In Maryland and Virginia some farms have stayed in the family for 14 and 15 generations, but in no case have they transferred directly from father to son all this time.

Hugh Tuttle, the head of this longest line of family farmers, stands tall, weathered, friendly, and proud of his heritage. He thinks that possibly the main reason that the farm remained in the direct line is that his ancestors up until two generations ago were staunch Quakers. A tenet in the Quaker church in his area was rather unusual. It dictated that the *youngest* son should inherit the farm. "I've never run into this anywhere else," he says.

Any older sons were given $100—if the family could scrape that much together—and sent into the world. If they ever returned, they were treated like boarders. They were expected to pay for their room and board. Hugh figures that having the youngest son inherit the farm was intended for the next generation. That is, the youngest son would be in the prime of life and better able to care for the elderly. There was no place to put the elderly in those days; families took care of them. Hugh's own great-great-grandfather had 27 mouths to feed—grandparents, maiden aunts, feeble-minded elderly.

The family farm is an enterprise a far cry from the old days. Today it is a popular roadside red-barn farm next to well-tended fields. In addition, plants and cut flowers are sold as well as grains and cereals and other health foods. It's a big business, something the old-timers in the family wouldn't recognize. At the same time, it is still the Tuttle family farm, well over three centuries old—and this is what Hugh talks about.

Did the original John Tuttle come here for religious reasons? To get away from persecution?

I don't think so. Most of those who came for religious reasons settled down in the Massachusetts Bay Colony. Most of them were protesting the rigors of the then very firm Church of England. He was an apprentice barrelmaker in Bristol. It was a seven-year apprenticeship and all you got was a garret to sleep in somewhere and some kind of slop to eat. About the fourth year of apprenticeship he figured he wasn't going to go through all that and when he got done all he got was making barrels for a dollar a day.

This was the last years of the reign of Charles I, two or three years before he lost his head. They were just trying to populate the New World with anybody willing to sign his name or make an X. John Tuttle made his X and was given parcel number 14 on Hilton's Point. This was Hilton's Point. Now it's Dover Point. The original settlement is two miles down the road. They had come over here in 1623, nine years previously, and established a settlement right on the point where the arch bridge is now. It was an ideal location because they had water on three sides. They had only one border to protect from Indians. They had navigable water and had to live off the water for years. There was a solid stand of white pine timber here. No land to begin with. So they were living off the water—fish and shellfish. All the transportation was by water. And it wasn't until 20 or 30 years later that they built a very primitive road up to Dover where the waterfall was because somebody had grown enough grain and they needed a grist mill. There was no running water on Dover Point to impound to use for running a mill. So somebody built a grist mill up there and the settlement stayed down here. But gradually people migrated up around the grist mill, which became a cotton mill and so on, a typical development of a New England mill town.

FAMILY FARMING

When did the family actually start cutting down the timber to make some farmland?

Obviously, they must have done it almost immediately because they couldn't live entirely off the production of the water. They had to grow some grain. It was a purely self-sufficient existence. It must have been terrible those first few years. How they ever did it I don't know.

Of course, they just slashed them down and burned them. Built their log cabins out of some of the best, burned the rest, and farmed around the stumps. They couldn't get the stumps out; they just had to let them rot.

Which took years and years.

You know, many people have this dream of wanting to get in a time machine and show up on earth here 50 years or 100 years from now. I would like to come back and see what it was like, oh, maybe five or ten years after my ancestor arrived. I think I know how bad it was when he arrived, but I'd like to see how much theywere able to accomplish with nothing but the very simplest of handtools. Most of the people, like him, had virtually nothing. So theyobviously didn't have draft animals. They had to buy an old scrubcow and raise a cow, grow it into an ox, and put him to work.

Do you have any hint about what tools they had at that time? Because it was a new life totally from scratch. In fact, they must have literally scratched out a living.

We don't have any tools that date back that far. I have an awful lot of antique tools, but they date to about 1840 or 1850. They must have had some kind of axe. I can't imagine what they did with those enormous pines. It must have taken two days to chop one off the stump.

In those days they were giant pines, too.

Apparently, they were enormous. There were mast roads everywhere in this area. They just top-graded all the woodlots and took the beautiful straight trees, hauled them out and floated them down to Portsmouth and shipped them over to the King's navy. So this was one of the worst problems, that they started out top-grading the wood lots, and we've just reversed that trend in the last four years. Prior to that we were always taking out the best and leaving the junk. Now we're going to reverse direction. Of course, the interest in burning wood for heat now is helpful because that provides a market for the junk.

Were these people who first came over literate? Could they read and write? Are there any surviving letters, for instance?

We don't know. The old family Bible starts with the records kept in the fourth or fifth generation. There's nothing written prior to that. His name appeared on the settlement records in 1636. We don't know actually when he arrived because he was shipwrecked off the coast of Maine on the way over. They ran into a hurricane and got washed ashore. Navigation wasn't too good back then, and he had to find his way overland.

Of course, this was a comparatively benign area as far as Indians were concerned. There weren't too many, and they were just passing through. But I cleared some land of timber that had never been plowed. It sat right on the bank of the Bellamy River, and the topsoil was only about 5 or 6 inches thick. (That's what white pine *won't* do for you compared to the prairie grass of Iowa.) But in the process of plowing we struck what looked to me like an old oyster bed. It was a dump, an Indian dump, because we found arrowheads. They had come down to the coast on the bank of this salt river and obviously had built a dam, closed it at high tide, and sat around and ate oysters and fished while it evaporated. They had their year's supply of salt, and then they went back inland somewhere.

With the tall stand of white pine there was almost no wildlife here either. Very little. Oh, some rabbits. Very few deer. In fact, we never saw a deer here until about 75 or 100 years ago, so my ancestors told me.

What do you think were some of the values that John Tuttle and the others who came over here had that made them so persistent and eventually successful? Obviously, they established their farm and a whole new life. Are those same values still around, maybe in a different form, or not?

Oh, yes, I think they are, but they're manifested in a completely different way. These entrepreneur-achiever types would have been ideally suited probably. You have to remember, we're looking at a completely different viewpoint of what these early settlers went through. What they had in England wasn't any better. There was oppression, terribly grinding poverty, enough of a caste system—if you were born of nobility that was your right, but you couldn't ascend to it from the ranks.

We tend to forget that.

Yes, yes. There was the opportunity in the New World. Even as horrible and backbreaking as this must have been, it was still better than what they had come from. If you make barrels for four years for nothing!

His wife's name was Dorothy. We don't know if she came over after they were married. We don't even know what her family name was. There were always children, but, in fact, my generation, and my children's generation, is the first where there was only one boy. So there was no test before. We went through the test because my son said "no way." It was going to be the end of the line. But back he came. And he now has one son.

The pressure was on the Tuttles to carry on the family farm and keep it in direct line from father to son. At first, Hugh's son Bill was not wild about carrying on the farm. About 1972 he went to Tufts University, majored in sociology, and was interested in prison reform. He drifted into various jobs to help out with his college education, selling used cars on the side. He ended up as the top salesman on the East Coast while working for a Buick and Cadillac dealer in Boston.

He was a natural merchandiser, Hugh says, not a farmer at all and with none of the growing instincts that Hugh has. Eventually, Bill went to work with Campbell Soup Company, but in the end he got fed up with the commuting and living in suburbia, Hugh says. One nice spring morning he came home to work for the farm.

Hugh sees that, although the growing instincts were left out of his son, they jumped a generation to his grandson. At five and a half, he's always carrying bugs in his hand or frogs in his pockets, and he helps out in the field. And naturally Hugh nudges the instinct along while Bill concentrates on selling what he grows.

What about some of the previous generations? Was the land exposed to some of the wars that came through here in the early days of the country?

I don't think so. We were not really affected by the Revolutionary War. In each instance, my direct-line ancestor was not involved in any military operations. They were Quakers, of course. I had numerous relatives who were involved in various wars down through the years. This was a kind of backwater area during the Revolutionary War. The Civil War didn't affect us greatly, although some of my relatives were killed in the Civil War.

Were any buildings destroyed in any way?

No, the worst destruction we've had is the torching of a gorgeous old kettle barn right across the street from the farmhouse. That was 12 years ago, a couple of kids. They went on a barn-burning spree. They burned 22 or 23 old hand-done barns in the area, the old barns that were raised with all the neighbors coming to help, the joints with the hardwood pegs to hold them together. Ah, it was brutal. It was a beautiful building.

Are there any 1600s buildings or remnants still here?

No. The sill of the original log cabin is still buried in the front lawn of the farmhouse. My son lives there now; we live

FAMILY FARMING

across the street. They obviously built a one-room log cabin and then added onto it. The original immigrant John had five children, and from there it seemed to go to seven and eight and nine and ten in every generation. They lived in the log cabin while they built the present house, which was built about 1770, 1780. They lived in the log cabin for 140 years. Probably upgraded it some. I suspect it was still a dirt floor. Privvy out back, which was standard in those times.

No refrigeration and air conditioning either.

No. I'm 62 now. The things you're writing about fascinate me because in my youth we were still doing all those old things. We operated a little pond where we cut ice with all the horse-drawn ice-cutting equipment. All through the neighborhood everybody had their little icehouse. Then, in the house where I grew up prior to 1921 when rural electrification finally got down here, we had the dumb waiter that went down into the basement. We'd put a keg of ice in once a week, these big 100-pound cakes out of the icehouse. The old icehouse is still standing; it's used for storage but not storage of ice. You'd lower the milk and the cream and butter and cheese down the dumb waiter. It went down into an insulated box right next to the keg of ice. Now my son uses the dumb waiter to bring firewood up from the basement. And the kids ride up and down.

What about the land itself? Has it changed from the early days?

Obviously, it had to have changed, but through a freak of nature my ancestor drew probably the best piece of land in 20 miles. Geologically, it's an old river delta. Prior to the ice age there was a single river here, not the two that meet three miles down the road. We're on a hogback in between. There was a single river and we're about 40 feet above sea level now, but the ocean was about 40 feet higher. You go two miles down at Dover Point and it's clear marine clay. So the first settlers drew parcels of marine clay, but my ancestor drew a lot far enough up, sight unseen, and it happened to be light sandy soils, which you find only in the river valleys here in New Hampshire. No stones.

There isn't a stone wall on the farm. You see, we were too close to sea level. All we got was the silt and the sand. You go another 15 miles inland, the big rocks dropped out as the glacier melted when it hit the ocean. The big stuff dropped out first, then the medium size, and we got the outwash right at the beach level.

So your ancestors were very fortunate.

They weren't fighting the boulders, and the topsoil was naturally deeper. They drew a much better than average chunk of land and I suspect that this is probably the reason that they hung on while the others moved west. All the guys that drew the rock piles, you know, after a generation, they said to hell with it.

I have a saying that if the United States had been flopped over and the early settlers had hit the coast of California instead of New England, we probably wouldn't have bothered to find New England yet. There was no reason to move because there was the soil and the weather and everything right there. Certainly, New England would be very different. We wouldn't recognize it. There wouldn't be any mill towns and I suspect that it would be much like the West; it would be primarily federally owned and for recreation.

What size lot did the early settlers usually get?

We don't really know. It was just described as parcel number 14 and nobody's ever seen the map from which the parcels were drawn on. The early descriptions were "the big stone and two rods from the big tree"—and so everything is long since gone. We think it was probably somewhere around 15 acres. The family acquired more, I acquired land, but now we're at a stopping point because this is now the desirable place to live, Dover Point is.

The particular lay of the land around Dover Point gives it a lot of water frontage. This in turn generates a natural air conditioning, with the bay area 8 to 10 degrees cooler in summer, 8 to 10 degrees warmer in winter than Dover three miles away.

All this and more makes Dover increasingly expensive. House lots cost $25,000. Hugh remembers that somebody bought two acres on the river for $190,000 for the land only. "It's a world I don't even know about," he says.

The Tuttle farm itself has 245 acres total now. This is very close to the national average for farms. Hugh bought 36 acres back in 1956. The cost per acre then was $100.

It's also a world that his ancestor would never recognize. A little later, Hugh quietly laments the loss of the personal touches with customers at the farm. The Tuttle enterprise has grown so large that hired clerks who come and go don't know anything of the long family history. It's similar to the lament he has for the 1940s when the supermarkets eliminated the small Mom and Pop markets, the ones that carried their customers through the Depression but were left with debts and out in the cold. "Now the supermarkets are starting to imitate the roadside farms," he said. "Now they're 'farm-fresh'!"

Obviously, you live in a very special place. What does it mean that you live on this piece of land?

A sense of tradition has to grow with you as you mature and get older. It didn't have any real significance to me as a kid; it has very little for my children, they still aren't impressed by it. I'm getting to the point where I'm pretty impressed.

My father lived to a ripe old age, he lived to his late eighties, and he was so wrapped up in it that he wrote an amateurish type family history with some of the old family stories. When you come from a long tradition like this, there's a whole lore, the family stories, the incidents, some funny, some sad, some just typical of the times. Sayings of the old-timers. And we try to preserve them. Some are unique to us. For instance, we call a three-day-old storm a Hummock storm, and it all dates back to probably four generations ago when the Quakers had their quarterly meetings, a regional meeting when Quakers from 30 miles around would come to a single meeting house. So the local families put up all those who came in and our family happened to draw the Hummocks. The Hummocks were an elderly couple with no children, and this

A sense of tradition has to grow with you as you mature and get older. It didn't have any real significance to me as a kid; it has very little for my children, they still aren't impressed by it. I'm getting to the point where I'm pretty impressed.

storm hit. The Hummocks were stern Quakers and felt that children should be seen and not heard. So the poor kids had to sit around the house and not play or anything, just sit there and be polite. They dreaded the Hummocks coming anywhere, but a three-day stand to the Tuttles is now a Hummock!

Ah, that's good. Has your land been exhausted at all?

No, the land is getting better all the time. Fortunately, it was good to begin with, by comparison. It wasn't Iowa but it was good.

My ancestors had some instincts for stewardship; we call it soil conservation now, but they had a stewardship in that I think they recognized with a strong Quaker base that they were merely stewards and the next generations would have to survive off the same land. So they didn't bleed it like so many others did who stayed only a little while and moved on. They were deeply rooted right from the beginning. We didn't have an extension service, no USDA, we had nobody to tell us what to do in those days. But they made maximum use of animal manures, they used their wood ashes. I suspect they adopted the Indian methods of burying dead fish for fertilizer. And, of course, they were absolutely right; there's nothing better than dead fish.

I can remember as a small child helping my father and grandfather blend fertilizer. Now, commercial fertilizer is a new phenomenon, it only came along in the mid-twenties. At that time you could not buy a bag of 5-10-10. You could buy a bag of ground phosphate rock, and you could buy muriate of potash, which is a mined product, and you could buy Chilean nitrate of soda, which is a naturally mined nitrogen product. They'd come in these enormous 200-pound bags and we'd dump them out and make a cake out of it, all the layers of these ingredients, and mix it with hoes and then bag it up. My grandfather was way ahead of his time. He was an avid reader and made fertilizers for specific plants. It was subsistence agriculture: produce all you can and barter for what you can't produce. I remember as a child sitting down at the dinner table and my father saying that the only things that weren't produced here on the farm are the salt and pepper.

Fantastic.

We had some chickens, ducks, beef cattle, dairy, we raised some pigs every year. My father was a great hunter and could bring in a deer or two. In those days, two were legal and three if you could manage it! So I grew up in a subsistence existence. My kids don't know what it is and it's a crying shame.

Yes, that's another point. How does that whole family line of subsistence living fit into today's living? How do you view it? Are we really advancing, or are we not? Is it better today?

I don't think it's better. I don't like it. We've become well into an age of specialists—one-track-mind types. A guy that can drive left-handed nails onto the left-handed side of the building. I can do almost anything because I grew up on subsistence farming. I'll dress out beef, milk a cow, dress a hog. I can carpen, I can plumb, I can weld, I can do most anything. Because you *had* to do most anything on the farm. I had to learn all those trades. But some don't know one end of the hammer from the other. It saddens me, it bothers me. I had chores; I had to milk two cows every morning and night.

Do you see anything switching back at all?

Well, you see a back-to-nature trend, but they're all freaky types, I'm sorry to say. There're an awful lot of people who want to stop the world and get off, you know, but they can't make a living at it, not by today's standards. They can provide a standard of living for themselves according to what my ancestors knew 100, 150 years ago, but that's no longer good enough. You don't want to use a privy on a cold winter morning. You're expected to send your kids to college and you can't do it by subsistence farming. It would be very difficult for today's young people, even though they yearn for the past. They haven't lived with the past; I have.

Prior to when electricity first came, we had a gravity water system and we were better off than most. The well was higher than the house. On Sunday night, the water circulated through a water jacket in front of the wood stove in the kitchen. Saturday night was bath night and before we sat down for dinner, my mother would go upstairs and turn on the faucet. The three-quarters-of-an-hour meal was just enough time for that tub to get full, but that was the one tank of hot water for the day. So first my older brother would get in, then I'd get in, then my little brother would get in, then my little sister. By the time we got through, the tub looked like coffee! No, you can't return to those days.

Do you want to?

I don't want to. I remember what they were like. I remember getting out of bed on a winter morning with no heat in the bedrooms, 16 down cushions over you and you'd plant your feet on the floor and there'd be ice in the wash basin, this sort of thing.

_____

As a child, Hugh saw the original land grant. It was still readable. He remembers the beautiful scrolls and fancy lettering and he remembers his father pointing out Charles I's signature. It was just a scribble. Sometime in the early part of this century, the land-grant document was lost.

The Tuttle farm was partly a dairy farm until 60 years ago. Hugh Tuttle took over the farm in 1953; his father retired three years later. In 1965, he and his wife started selling the farm produce retail. They had about 35 acres of cropland then, and he cleared and leveled more land, some of it swampland. It was hard work, but the work ethic wasn't dead then as he finds it now.

_____

If you could give one thunderbolt point of what you've learned being on this unique farm, what would it be?

It is a sense of roots. That's what's grabbing so many people now, they're searching for their roots. Some of the younger generation express it as trying to find themselves, get my head together. But a sense of belonging. With the kind of nomadic society we have today—my God, I know people who move every two years, jumping from job to job, location to location with the same company. They have no sense of security. I walk out across the fields, and I say that nine generations of Tuttles have put their feet in the same place. I wonder what they think of what we're doing because it's so different. I know they disapprove of some of the things we're doing. We're a little too profit-motivated.

This has always been a one-family farm, but suddenly I had three kids returning all with twentieth-century expectations. So we tried to turn it into a four-family farm and we had to make some compromises like being open year-round. The thing I like about my side of the business is that I'm still seasonal. I'm very adapted to the seasons; I'm a child of Mother Nature. I'm geared to seasons. It's very important.

Maybe some of your ancestors would disapprove of some things. But do you think they would approve of what you're doing?

I'm sure they would approve of the way we're managing the land, managing the wood lot. But they'd look around and say, "What has thee done? There's no place for cows anymore!" This would not be a farm to them—the store—but we're taking care of the land.

Also, your ancestors must approve that you kept the farm in the family name.

Oh, yes, this would please them mightily. Yep.

PRINCESS RED WING

Living as a Narragansett

Princess Red Wing of Seven Crescents

Exeter, Rhode Island

Before the non-Indian settlers edged into this country, the Narragansetts were the largest and strongest tribe in southern New England, stronger than all the neighboring tribes of the Mohegans, Pequots, Niantics, Cowesetts, Nipmucs, and Wampanoags. Many of the customs and habits of New England—and, for that matter, of the whole United States of North America—can be traced to the influence over the centuries of these native Americans.

Today about 1,000 Narragansetts live in Rhode Island, but their heritage is felt far more than their numbers. For many years Princess Red Wing has been one who points out and reminds non-Indians of this special heritage. At 87 years of age, she is articulate, strong-voiced and strong-minded, quick-eyed and friendly, not to mention her radiant smile.

She is a legend in her area. In her lifetime she has published a Narragansett newspaper, given tours, lectured across the country, been a member of a research group for the United Nations from 1947 to 1970, and in just about every other way has told the story of the Narragansetts. Now she is curator of the Tomaquag Indian Memorial Museum in Arcadia Village in Exeter.

She wears a beaded headband, many silver bracelets, and a colorful blouse and dress as we talk in the front room of the museum.

What did you speak about for the UN? What did you do there?

Oh, about UNICEF and big issues that came up in the General Assembly. I was in the General Assembly when Marshall gave his speech on what became the Marshall Plan. I guess I met everybody there because I was the only American Indian they came up with. "Can I take you to cocktails? Can I take you to lunch? Can I have your picture for my paper? What does the Indian think of this, what does the Indian think of that?"

You must have seen a lot of changes during your life. What are some of these big changes, some of the changes among your people around here?

Of course, their reservation was bought in 1880 and they were made citizens of the state and citizens of the United States. Back when my grandmother had to go to school, they had a school but the non-Indians said it wasn't up to par so send the Indian children to public school. Well, a group of people took over that old Indian school and that went on until the last member, and the club asked that that old school go back to the Narragansett tribe. But they didn't give it to the tribe; they gave it to the YMCA in Providence and they did nothing with it. Vandalism tore it down. Then the people of Charlestown rose up. They knew that they had not only the oldest school intact in the state but in the United States. Because these people kept every board up, everything intact like it was when the Indians went to school back in the early 1800s. Then they started the Charlestown Historical Society to save other old things. I've been historian for that society.

Did you attend that school?

No, no, that was back in my grandmother's time.

Did you live here as a child in this area?

I was born in Connecticut. I was five years old when they brought us over here.

Have you seen over the years an improvement of Indian rights?

Yes, because more have been educated. Help Indians to higher education and then they become a help to society rather than a menace. I recommended Phil to go to school, but he didn't want to leave home, but his brother Ferris said he would go. I talked to all the clubs, made a circuit, and they paid his tuition and books. Well, he came through and for 22 years he was moderator of the town of Exeter, 19 years supervisor at General Dynamics at Groton, and owned and operated Dovecrest and started it here. He only passed away this last March. Now I say, you're helping Indians with higher education. He was the oldest of eight children. His mother never could have sent him through all of this. Then I got older and I came to live with them. So I said, now Ferris, I took care of you, now you take care of me! I've lived with them since 1960.

I understand that some land has been given back to the tribe recently.

Yes, that's right. You know, they declared that it wasn't a tribe in 1880 when the reservation was sold. The tribe broke up. Well, I was just out of the hospital and I couldn't testify, but they said Red Wing can remember! Anything they wanted to know, ask Red Wing. So they brought all their apparatus down from the court. I said, yes, I can remember back over 80 years when my father used to come to the tribal meeting. I was a little shaver, I said, and my mother was from another tribe. So he'd come home and tell my mother the tribe did this, the tribe did that. Of course, I wanted to know what a tribe was. I didn't know whether it was an animal or what it was. What's a tribe, what's a tribe, mother? My mother explained to me that a tribe was people with Indian blood. That turned the trick for the whole land that they got down there, because I could remember further back than any of the others when it was tribal.

Have some of the traditions changed from when you were young?

Yes, because all the old-timers are gone. Before the old-timers were gone we used to have big tribal meetings, sometimes 100 there. Now I've been down to some of the tribal meetings and it's 25 or 30, one or two trying to run everything. So after I married White Oak he says, Get out of that tribe, Red Wing, don't try to carry it on your shoulders anymore. Go out and do your lectures, get your money, and come home. I can't be bothered about giving up an evening and arguing about this and arguing about that—"She's more Indian than he is"—because they're all mixed.

Then I gave Indian dance classes. I spent 28 years teaching in summer camps, not Indians, but young Americans, lovely things, and then I gave it up and I started the campfire programs in Charlestown. I gave them every week and the town clerk said, Oh, don't stop, Red Wing, because everybody's missing it. Of course, everybody used to enjoy coming to those campfire programs. I knew that the thing the children enjoyed was the good times the children had around the campfires. So I said, I'll start these programs so the children who hadn't been to camp can see how much fun it is. Sometimes I'd have a hundred people around those campfires. They came from all over everywhere. I'd do it for eight weeks and have a different subject for each week so they'd come to all of them. I had this group of Indian children do the dances accordingly for each one, and I'd ask all of them which ones would like to get up into the round dance and try it.

What would be some of the subjects you'd talk about?

Well, the subjects would be on the different ceremonies, their clothes, their foods, their crafts, things like that, all their different ideas.

For instance, what would you talk about for their foods?

For the foods, I'd have johnnycakes, of course, and like I say, five-sevenths of what's on our American tables today the Indians had before the settlers ever reached these shores. Your potatoes, your corn, your beans, your squash, your pumpkin, your melon. It wasn't until 1850 the tomato went on the American table. Old-time settlers said, Don't eat that, it's poison! The Irish potato came from America, flourished in Ireland and that's what they raised, but it came from America first. Pineapple in Hawaii came from further south here in America, got over there and people think it started over there, but it started over in America. People think that the Italians started the tomato for their spaghetti, but the tomato didn't go around the world until after 1880. Because one person ate the tomato and lived!

The herbs! When the children come here—they come by the busloads from Connecticut, Rhode Island, Massachusetts—I say to the children, How many of you have had a wild cherry cough drop? Some young one will pop up, I did, I did. Well, I say, the Indians did, too, but they [the children] wouldn't understand rosemary and anisette and different herbs.

What about the ceremonies? What would you talk about at the campfires?

How they used the ceremonies for appealing to the Great Spirit for this or that or the other, you see. Ages ago they had a thanksgiving every moon to thank the Great Spirit for something. We've merged into civilization, but we still have five thanksgivings. Then in December we have the ceremony of Nickomo, of giving away. So they danced for the privilege of putting a gift into the circle for the less fortunate of the tribe. Last year we decided to invite the public to our Nickomo in December when the days are short and the nights are long, but we said that when you come bring something for somebody less fortunate than yourself. So we had a busload of things to distribute among the needy families in the south county. Then we said you have to dance now. We started the drummaker, we had a lot of fun with it. You can skip or jump or anyway you want, just so you dance. Just step to the beat of the drum, put your gift in the circle. We had a *pile* of things to give. People brought things like canned goods, children's mittens and stockings, sweaters, things like that, some brought toys for children, coloring books, all kinds of things they brought.

You said you had five thanksgivings. Now what would those be?

We've had our thanksgivings for the giving of the sweet of the maple sap. That comes in the second week in March. Our thanksgiving for the strawberry comes in the second Sunday in June. That's the nicest one of all because that's the thanksgiving of renewed friendships. Everybody makes up with everybody else, no matter how angry you are with your brother, your cousin, your neighbor. Nobody gets into the strawberry dance with a grudge or mad or angry. Everything is forgiven when you get into the strawberry dance.

Does it work?

I say, it's forgiven that day, even if they fight the next day! At least everybody is forgiven that day and at peace. Because, you see, the strawberry was given as a peace offering, that's why. And then the thanksgiving for the green bean. When they found out they could eat the green bean as well as the white bean, they had to have another thanksgiving for a new dish and that comes on the third Sunday in July.

Now our next thanksgiving is the thanksgiving for the cranberries. The Great Spirit looked after his children of the forest because they lived so close to nature and nature's garden. He knew some weren't as fast as their brothers and sisters, some were a little slower, and maybe even a little lazier, but he took pity on them just the same. And after the great frost, or a few cold days, he turned the warm winds back so they could be saved against the cold winter to get their harvest in. Because they were slower, you see. Now he gave them a berry, but he used all the sweetness in the raspberries, blackberries, strawberries, but they gathered their cranberries just the same, made up their cranberry juice, cranberry sauce, Indian cranberry bread, and on the first Saturday in October we thank the Great Spirit for the cranberries.

Now the thanksgiving for the harvest and the garden, the fields and the meadows, that's the one Squanto told the Pilgrims it was time to have. They didn't feel very festive when another cold winter was ahead of them, the crops were poor to begin with, out of 150 people some only about 52 or 53 were living when that first fall came around. Squanto stepped down to Plymouth and said to Governor Bradford, When things look dark, your crops are poor, many passing to the hereafter, that's the time for the biggest feast, the biggest thanks to your Creator to show him that you're not complaining against your hard lot.

Governor Bradford answered, That would be good for my fainting people, go call your people and tell them to come and we will thank God for what blessings we have. The Indians came with their wild turkeys, their deer meat, their potatoes, their beans, their squash, their pumpkins enough to feed all of Plymouth and themselves and they cooked it up and ate and thanked God. Now in schools they teach that that was the first

LIVING AS A NARRAGANSETT

Thanksgiving. To those Pilgrims it was, but to my ancestors it was just another thanksgiving for the harvest of the garden, the forests, fields, and meadows. And we celebrate that thanksgiving now in conjunction with the national Thanksgiving. That's the only one you have to have a reservation for, because we hold it in the dining room. The others are held out in the friendship circle.

Princess Red Wing has a son, Metacomet, who's a high school teacher in Tampa, Florida, and a daughter married and living in Warwick, Rhode Island. Her daughter's son lives in Ventura, California, and her daughter's daughter is married and lives in Mississippi. "So we're all over the country," she says.

At the time we speak, Princess Red Wing has a talk at the University of Connecticut on her list and is scheduled to speak at morning Sunday school and evening services for the Methodist Church. She says, "If you want me, send a car."

The rays of her spirit and energy emanate all over from her museum in Exeter. At one time she worked with Dr. Betty Rosenthal for two years in Massachusetts to help correct television programs on the American Indian. When Dr. Rosenthal moved to Arizona, she wanted to see Princess Red Wing, so Princess Red Wing went down to Arizona and brought back a piece of Hopi blue corn bread!

She leads a tour of her museum. The small size gives no hint whatsoever of the exquisite artifacts on display—finely crafted baskets, pipes, blankets, ceremonial clothing, tools, wampum. She explains it all with good stories and undying enthusiasm.

This is all so good. Are these good values of your ancestors pretty much alive, do you think?

Sometimes we have over 200 people to these thanksgiving ceremonies here. Indians and non-Indians come to them. Of course, there's the Indian's religion. Everybody's written something about their religion, they worship this and that. Well, the Indian here on the eastern seaboard never worshipped anything that he could conquer. He could make himself an abode and protect himself in the worst weather. He could lay under a tree or jump in the water to cool himself off. He could make weapons and kill the worst animals of all. He never worshipped anything that he could conquer. The sun, the moon, the stars, the wind, the animals, and *all* of nature was the Creator's way of speaking to and maintaining all of mankind and that was the basis of the Indian's religion. Every single morning my ancestor parted the doorway of his wigwam, went out on a hill, and talked with his Creator to ask for the wisdom of the day. Then his mate went out and his children went out and every single morning, summer and winter, they jumped into the water to cleanse their bodies. When a new baby was born, he was dunked, too, even if he was born in January. And I tell the children he was fortunate if he was born in June instead of January! Even if they cut a hole in the ice, he was dunked just the same! He got dunked. Make him strong. Because they always built their villages near a lake or a pond or a river or something because they had to use the water. They didn't have water in their wigwams.

How many teachers I've had to teach from Connecticut, Rhode Island, Massachusetts that all Indians didn't live in a teepee! I said to one teacher, I said, Even my ancestors didn't live in a teepee, they lived in a *wigwam*. "Isn't a wigwam and a teepee the same?" I said, Absolutely not. Wigwam is round like a half-ball, dome shaped, covered with bark. Out on the prairie, Cheyenne, Sioux, Blackfeet, Winnebago lived in teepees. They're the pointed ones, round, covered with leather. They can take up the poles, fold up the leather, and make the trip as they follow the buffalo. Farther out west they lived in hogans and pueblos made of clay and sand and whatever they had. Way up north they lived in igloos, way down south they lived in wickiups. They all did *not* live in teepees.

They all did not have canoes either. They had a dugout. I show them how they cut down a tree. The tree had to be big enough and wide enough for them to sit in. They do that by putting a wide piece of leather around that big tree. Keep it soaking wet. Then on the ground next to the tree they built a little fire and chopped that charred wood with a stone axe. Another little fire, another little fire, another little fire, and they

LIVING AS A NARRAGANSETT

keep doing it until they fell a big tree. Then they split it with their wedges and half of it they build a fire and scrape, fire and scrape, fire and scrape until they had a dugout. There's an authentic Indian dugout at the Haffenreffer Museum in Bristol, came out of the Ponagansett Pond in northern Rhode Island. The anthropologists say it was preserved down in the mud over the years.

Did your ancestors fish much in the bay, what's now Narragansett Bay?

Yes, they moved down to the seashore, gather all sorts of shellfish, wrap it in seaweed, put it over the hot coals to steam and that was the beginning of the Rhode Island clambake. And they caught all kinds of seafood. Then they moved back into the hills and made their journey cakes. The English liked those little journey cakes. They smoothed the *journey* down to *johnny*; now it's the Rhode Island johnnycakes.

What were some of the ways your ancestors taught their young?

See that bee's nest? I tell the children, See that bee's nest hanging there in the corner? At other museums you wouldn't see things like that. So I tell them, I say, They had no schools. How do I teach my children? They had to learn all their lessons from nature. The first lesson they taught their children was that obedience was the first law of happiness and success. They wouldn't have had a bee's nest that big—and some were bigger— they wouldn't have had one like that if all had not obeyed the queen bee and worked together. So from some of the littlest things in nature they learned some of their greatest lessons.

Then they saw how the ducks walked on the top of the snow with their feet. So they learned to make snowshoes because they learned they could get along faster if they walked on top of the snow instead of every step they took their foot went down 5 or 6 inches. So they had snowshoes ages and ages ago.

Ages and ages ago they had their clans. Head of the clans were the women, head of the nations were the men. When an Indian traveled into a strange village on the eastern seaboard, he looked for the sign of the clan to which he belonged. If he

When an Indian traveled into a strange village on the eastern seaboard, he looked for the sign of the clan to which he belonged. If he belonged to the turtle clan and he saw a turtle on a strange abode, he could find home, friends, food, and rest.

belonged to the turtle clan and he saw a turtle on a strange abode, he could find home, friends, food, and rest. If he belonged to the deer clan, or the wolf clan, he looked for that sign.

And they formed the first league of nations for peace here in America over a hundred years before the Revolutionary War, all over New England and New York and as far south as Virginia. After the Revolutionary War Thomas Jefferson and Benjamin Franklin went right to that league, studied their by-laws for the

Constitution of the United States of America. And Benjamin Franklin recorded, and it is recorded, "It seems strange that we need to go to the natives for our form of government." Across the waters they never heard of a government of the people and by the people. Here the Indians had a democratic government and they all voted. Women voted as well as the men, they didn't have to fight for women's suffrage and women's rights. The women were precious in the sight of native men. She was the mother of all understanding, she was the producer of the tribe, she was the mother of the clans. Anne Hutchinson was banished from Plymouth because she wouldn't worship the way they did. The Pilgrims came over for the freedom to worship God, but they gave it to nobody else. I tell the children, They couldn't take a bus in those days, they put her out and she had to travel among the natives and she settled among the Narragansetts and they recorded a native man never touched her disrespectfully, never said a disrespectful word, because ages ago womanhood was precious in the sight of the native men.

In ancient times these tribes banded together as a protection. There must have been some conflict with neighboring tribes. Was there much warfare among their neighbors?

Their warfare was more like contests. That creed we still teach to our children. Our fathers had many good laws that they learned from their fathers. They told us that we should never be the first to break a bargain, that we should treat all men as they treat us, that it was a disgrace to tell a lie, that we should never take from another his life or his property without paying for it with the same. The Great Spirit sees and hears everything and he never forgets, and he gives everyone a spirit home according to his just desserts. This I believe and this all my people believe the same. It's not too different from the Christian religion.

Yes, that sounds familiar. What do you think is your most proud work that you've done?

Well, I think my greatest work has been with children. I've mothered hundreds of motherless children away from home—white ones, black ones, Oriental ones, rich ones, poor ones, even the Vanderbilt twins—all away from home in the summer camps. I think that's my greatest work. Now I have busload after busload come here, sometimes busloads of three- and five-year-old nursery children. They're darlings. "What's that? How'd they do that?" I explain everything to them, talk to them, sit them down on the rug here, tell them legends and stories, take them out on the lawn and say, Come on now, step to the beat of my drum. It's wonderful.

I was speaking at the Meeting School in Providence, handicapped or something the matter with all of them there. Well, at that time I had a broken foot. I had 46 children. I had taken them over through the fish hatchery to show them some Indian herbs and to show them some of the natural things of life. I was looking at them, caught my foot on the root of a tree, fell forward, and broke my foot. So I had a cast up one foot. But I didn't stop. I had this lecture so I went. They put me in a wheelchair, took me around the school, and showed me everything. It's a beautiful school. Then I spoke to them. I said to them, You that don't have crutches and not in wheelchairs, get up on your feet and step to the beat of my drum. I began my drum. They got up and they did! Those people there at the school said nobody had kept the attention of those children as I did.

What would you most like to see happen in the near future for your people?

I'd like to see that they all have a good education. I say, help them in higher education to work in modern society.

What about the traditions and values of your people? What would you like most for them to keep?

I'd like them to keep their religion and their ceremonies because they lived closer to nature and nature's God and every single morning and day they lived with their Creator. I'd like them to keep their religion pure and clean.

I'm reading a book now that tells how awful they're treating Indians on reservations today and I wished they had higher education so they could fight that. It's like they put the Osage on

LIVING AS A NARRAGANSETT

the worst land they could find, said, If you red dogs can't live there, die there. What happened to them? The richest oil wells in the country came right up into their laps. Well, some of them are educated now and when companies come in and want to rip 'em off, they know enough to put them out and take some other company. That's what they need on all reservations, good schools and good education. Because on those reservations they cannot get their living when nature was their great storehouse of everything they wanted to eat and wear and build their abodes.

And look out there in Washington, how they're stopping the Indians with the salmon? Why, they could tell Washington how to preserve salmon. They've been preserving it all these thousands of years not to deplete the supply. Now Washington doesn't want them to fish. Why? Because they want the big fish companies to go out there and catch and eat it and sell it to the public. I told that big crowd out in Dallas that if the Indian there can't stop it, then you and you and you have got to stop it! If you want peace in your heart, you've got to lay aside your prejudices or you'll never have peace.

LEONARD SENDZIA

Lighthouse Keeping

Leonard Sendzia

North Truro, Massachusetts

If any area needs a lighthouse, it's sandy Cape Cod that hooks like a claw into the cold, stormy Atlantic. Highland Light is perched on the highest point on the Cape and is the oldest lighthouse in the area. First built in 1798, the lighthouse was constructed to help cut down the highest number of shipwrecks of any area on the East Coast. It was rebuilt in 1833 and then again in 1857 and is now operated by the U.S. Coast Guard. Senior Chief Leonard Sendzia is the officer in charge and, with Seamen Christopher Ordway and Ronald Barriere, he keeps the light operating 24 hours a day. Even today, with all the sophisticated electronic equipment on ships and boats, the lighthouse provides a vital function, especially on temperamental Cape Cod. Unlike the rocky coast farther up in Maine, the Cape is surrounded by shifting sandbars. Bitter northeast storms can throw ships off course and onto the beach, a disaster for lone fishermen as well as for cargo vessels. The last sizable shipwreck occurred at the turn of the century, but it was not like the last major disaster. That happened in 1853 in front of the light when 42 people died.

The light itself is one of the most powerful—4 million candlepower. Sometimes it's visible for 23 miles, depending on atmospheric conditions. On exceptional nights the light has been seen by fishermen leaving Maine and coming south. The actual light is 183 feet above the ocean.

Leonard obviously enjoys his work. He keeps the light and the grounds in sparkling condition, meets the curious people (especially in crowded summer), and sometimes gives tours (rangers from the Cape Cod National Seashore conduct regular tours). We talk of the famous Highland Light in the office before climbing to the revolving beam that has comforted and saved many a fortunate fisherman and captain.

———————————

A lighthouse station is more than just a light, isn't it?

Number one, it's the light. It's the first visible light coming across the ocean. By plane it's the first light they'll see going into Boston. We also have the radio beacon that transmits every six minutes. It's constantly on the air, 24 hours a day. Then we have a foghorn. When visibility drops to two miles, we turn on the foghorn. Anytime it's hazy, fogging, rainy, when visibility decreases, even snow, the foghorn is energized. The light is energized at the same time. So it's not just strictly that the light is on at night. It's a dual function. The vessels out there at sea can see the light in the haze and if they're in a cloud bank or haze, they know that visibility has decreased by seeing the light and also by listening for the horn.

What exactly does the light tell them?

Their position. Each light has its own characteristic. This light revolves every five seconds; it shows its light every five seconds. It's a double-drum light and it houses two 1,000-watt bulbs. Only one is lit at any given time. The second one in there is a backup in case the other one goes out. It automatically triggers the spare bulb into position immediately. The Nauset Light down the coast has a different characteristic. She flashes three every 10 seconds. Then you go around the Cape to Race Point, which is a 10-second and then Wood End, which is a flashing red every 10 seconds. Then at Long Point it's a fixed green light. So each one, as you look at the time cycle and at the chart, you can basically know which light you're looking at. They have stop watches to time the lights.

And these are found on a chart?

Oh, yes. This chart here is the same chart they'll use at sea. Here for Highland it says: It flashes 5 seconds, 183 feet, 23 miles;

it also has a foghorn and radio beacon on a frequency 286 which gives out a code signal H I in Morse Code. Four dots is the H, two the I.

When we turn the light on, we have a stopwatch and we'll start our watch going and watch the rotation of the light. We check the light ourselves every night that we're showing the proper characteristic.

Has it ever been off?

Well, in the two and a half years that I've been here we've only had to readjust it once and that was because we had an electrical problem. The light was out for about two hours, which was very rare. It was a faulty switch. We replaced it and we were back on.

Fishermen must use the light all the time.

All the fishermen use it and any ship that uses the area uses the light. It's a quick reference point. Any disaster that happens on the back side—when I say back side I'm talking about the ocean side compared to the bay, this is the ocean side here—we'll get, for example, a fishing boat taking on water. They'll always use Highland as a reference point. They'll say six miles northeast of Highland Light, or whatever. They also have a light list that gives more information; it'll give the latitude and longitude of a particular light you're looking for. Each light is listed by number. Ours is number 53. They go to the list and the number, and it'll tell them the height of the light, the candlepower, what its flashing characteristic is, what color the light is, how deep the water is, how high the antenna is, the latitude and longitude. One volume takes in the whole Atlantic coast. Also, our foghorn gives one blast every 15 seconds.

Is this lighthouse ever going to be automated?

No. Number one, it is historical. Number two is that it's such a tourist attraction and in a highly populated area that if there wasn't someone here to maintain the light, it would be vandalized. There's no doubt about that. There are others on the Cape that are automated and they show the vandalism signs. They're broken into. They take locks, they break windows. And it costs a lot of money to keep this up against the vandalism. And this is what would happen if Highland was ever automated. We constantly find people inside our yard.

Before this one was electrified, was it operated by gas?

It was first operated by whale oil. The lighthouse keeper made sure that everything was going right all night long. It had a Fresnel lens, which was built in France, that magnifies the light. At first it was all whale oil, then they had candles, then it progressed to kerosene, and to the electric stage. Now, just to make sure that nothing happens in case the power fails, we have an electrical generator. As soon as the power is interrupted, the generator automatically kicks on and keeps us in operation. There are alarm systems set up in the houses. There's an alarm in this house, plus outside alarms, so that if anything would happen an alarm switch is set for the house who's on duty. If that beacon goes out, that alarm sets off. It's very shrill, high-pitched. Most recently, lightning struck and burned out the foghorn and because it was so close, it did something to the radio beacon. It threw it out of its sequence. It was off by two minutes, and ships depend on that.

Obviously, that happened during a storm, so it was very important to get those back on.

Yes, but even if there was no storm, we have to get it back as soon as possible. The beacon runs in between other radio beacons and if it's off time and runs on another beacon's time, you'll have two beacons running at once and screw everything up. We share beacons with Duck Island, Ambrose down in New York, Nantucket, and four other stations that transmit on the same frequency as us, but it's broken down. We transmit every six minutes. So we transmit on the hour, 6 minutes, 12, 18, 24, and so on. The other one might transmit every two minutes on the second minute but every six minutes after. So they would go 2, 8, and so on. And another one would go every three minutes. You're on for one minute. We'll transmit for one minute and then we'll shut down. It's all done automatically. Then it's monitored by Boston that the proper signal is going out at the proper time. We monitor ourselves and we're also being monitored by another radio station as a backup.

We look through the 3-inch-thick, green-covered list that includes all vital information about lighthouses on the Atlantic coast. Then Leonard leads the way up the 79 steps of the 60-foot white tower to the light itself. The inside of the tower is immaculately clean and anything that can shine shines—brass knobs and plates especially. The iron footsteps with the original 1857 wooden railing spiral upward like the inside of an elongated seashell.

Our voices and steps echo up and down the tower. Toward the top we edge through a hole in the steel-plated floor of the light and, standing upright, we're at once in a warm, quiet, glass-enclosed room with a 360-degree view. The day is spectacular, with visibility unlimited. No need for the light, or for the foghorn stationed in sight below by the edge of the sandy, eroding, avalanche-prone cliff. Being the highest point on Cape Cod with unobstructed views, both sides of the peninsula can be seen. On the close side, the sandbars below the water surface are visible.

The light is a huge double-beam system of cut glass. Leonard opens the lens that magnifies the mercury vapor bulbs (each lamp costs $46 and lasts about six months as long as no one touches it with oil on his hands; special gloves and safety shields are put on before handling the bulbs).

To one side a local golf course can be seen. One of the most popular questions from the public is, What are those things over there that look like giant golf balls? Do they advertise the golf course? No, they're Air Force radar domes.

Lighthouse keeping can be filled with routine, and sometimes the routine needs some diversion. The story is told that at the nearby Chatham Light (of course, not at the Highland Light!), the seamen on duty had a certain way of turning on the light. Just as a tour of the grounds for the public arrived at the outside base of the tower, the guide would say, "Now they're just about to turn the light on." Then another seaman would go up to the tower, angle his leg back, and kick the tower. Immediately, the light above would flick on!

Down through the ages, as the four different sources of light have changed and become more automated, have the duties of the lighthouse keeper diminished?

Not really. The lighthouse itself has its own distinguishing characteristics also. It has a white tower; it's got to be kept white; it's got to be painted. There are others with different colors. Sometimes up on Newfoundland where they get snow, it wouldn't make sense to have a white tower against the snow background. One up there is painted completely red, although it has the white light. It's highly visible, as well as the light itself. Others are candy-striped, some are black. In order to paint this light, we use four people. Once a year. The winter snows take their toll. The sand blows off the cliff and if the storm is severe enough it'll give it a sandblasting effect. It will discolor to where it no longer looks white.

What about the light itself? Is there much maintenance needed?

You have to make sure there are two good bulbs in there. The glass has to be cleaned. Not keeping the windows clean cuts down on the intensity of the light. You usually clean them once a week or sooner if it's needed. They have to be cleaned outside as well as inside. And the outside lens, too.

There's a system of ducts where the light is, a natural flow of air, to keep the inside windows from fogging up. It kind of defrosts the windows, especially in winter. It's plain hot when you go up there.

That's a point. Is there more need for a lighthouse in the summer or winter?

You need one all the time, but in the winter you have snow, rain, a lot more than in the summertime. I'd say that the foghorn

You have to make sure there are two good bulbs in there. The glass has to be cleaned. Not keeping the windows clean cuts down on the intensity of the light. You usually clean them once a week or sooner if it's needed. . . . outside as well as inside.

is on more in the winter than the summer, but it's needed all the time. I'd say that if you look in the log, you find the foghorn on more in the winter, but you do get a lot of fog in the summer. In winter you get a lot of snow.

Does it need more maintenance in the winter?

It's very hard to do some of the things in winter that we do in the summertime. For example, the cleaning of the glass on the

LEONARD SENDZIA

outside. That's a hazard. Now for me to have one of these guys to go up in the winter. . . . I'll concede that much, because for them to take up these solutions and clean the windows, you create an ice barrier around your feet as you try to do it. Plus the wind blows up there constantly during the wintertime. It's nothing for the wind to be blowing at 25 and 30 knots. With that and the cold comes a high chill factor. We've had signs blown through windows in winter. A storm has blown a chainlink fence down. That snow packed up against it. It just blew it right down!

Is this area known for such storms?

Oh, yes. You know, Thoreau mentioned Highland four times and how powerful the winds were. He even stayed at the lighthouse. The winds are very strong.

Does the snow ever pack onto the light?

No, the wind won't let it, it blows so hard. Either that or if it packs on the glass it won't last long because the light'll heat it up and melt it off.

Are there ships out there during times like that?

There might be. We don't know. The light has a 23-mile range, but when the wind and snow really blow you may not see it. I've seen foggy weather so severe you couldn't see the house next door. You had to come up almost to that cliff down there to see this light. But the light keeps going.

BOB SPECKMAN AND JERRY

Clearing Land with Horses

Bob Speckman

Antrim, New Hampshire

Bob Speckman's modest barn-red house is perched on a cleared hilltop. Outside, the view pulls the eye to a long stretch of hills toward the heavily wooded northwest. Inside, the King cabinet-style wood stove sits to the side of the kitchen and we sit at the oval table where Bob puts down *The Draft Horse Journal*, published in Waverly, Iowa. It covers the news about work horses—Belgians, Percherons, Clydesdales, Shires, and Suffolks.

He's a soft-spoken man, the kind geared to working on his own and outdoors, knowing firsthand the sweat and solitude of it all. He wears a blue-brown plaid flannel shirt, green work pants, boots to ward off the mud season. Born in Keene, New Hampshire, about 30 miles from here, he's well part of the country around him. He has worked horses since he was 16, and he's part of them, too.

In the late 1950s, however, he broke off, packed up, and moved to California for a few years. He worked with horsepower there, but it was with a Lincoln-Mercury dealer in the San Francisco Bay area. Working with cars wasn't the same, especially the year he was transferred three times in one school year, which meant his kids were transferred, too.

"I said to hell with it," he recalls, "I'm going back to New England."

So here he is since returning in 1960. He took up where he left off, and he's been working with draft horses to clear woodlots for lumber and acreage for houses. It's hard work, but he likes working with horses, always has, and he likes being on his own. It's the right way to treat the land, not gouging and gashing it with diesel-spitting tractors, earth-scarring skidders, and hacked-out access roads. He feels good about liking what he does and doing it right, besides.

————————

How did you learn to use horses for clearing land in the first place?

My father did it before me. That was back when they had portable sawmills; they took them to the lot. He had six or eight horses then. He logged them right into the mills. They didn't truck them in those days, you know. As a matter of fact, I started when they had portable mills.

You've seen some changes then.

Oh, yes. As a kid I can remember the old steam mill. My father with the horses moved the boiler in by the mill. Of course, they put the mill in the middle of the lot so the logging would all be fairly short.

How much do you clear in a year? Or do you work by seasons?

Normally, we work year-round. Last winter the snow was so deep we finally quit. It wasn't just the deep snow. There was a crust on it and it was tough on the horses' legs. So we just quit for about two months.

Is it easier to work in winter?

The snow does make it easier on the horses for pulling the load.

You clear for houses but mostly it's for lumber.

Right, for logs. It depends on the size for houses, on whether it's a five-acre lot or a 100-acre lot. The one in Hopkinton is 45 acres. There's a lot of old growth timber on it. It'll take me, oh, I've been there two months and I guess I'll be there another two.

How much can you take out in a day?

About a truckload. About 4,000 feet. It goes on those cherrypicker trucks. Pine averages about 10 pounds to the foot. In other words, if you've got 4,000 feet on a truck, you've got about 40,000 pounds net weight. You take one log with, say, 300 feet in it, that's about a ton and a half. It's a pretty good load for the horses.

Why do you do it with horses? Why not let Detroit do it?

Well, for several reasons. One being I enjoy working with horses. I've done it all my life. And the second being that there are so many people today that get gun-shy of these skidders and tractors, the way they tear up the woods, make deep ruts, and cause erosion. Consequently, if a person thinks enough of their property to selectively cut and keep the young growth protected, they generally will sell their growth to someone with horses like me cheaper than they will sell it to a man with skidders that's going in there and ruin the place. Naturally, we don't do as much volume with a pair of horses as skidders do and we have to buy the wood cheaper.

Clearing with horses is the old tried and true way. But have you found over the years that people are still looking to what you do?

Oh, definitely. More all the time. A lot of people after they've seen skidder operations say there's no way they'll cut their lumber. Then they hear of someone like myself and I'm always glad to take them to some of the lots I've done. They change their thinking usually and go ahead and have me do it.

Basically, you cut the trees the same way.

Yes, but with skidders they cut the tree whichever way it leans and let it go and if it takes down three or four little ones, well, too bad. With horses, we put our main road in. Then we wedge the tree so that it'll go the way it should so you're pulling straight out on it and not around corners and knocking things over. The whole operation is just a much neater job.

Are some of these people thinking that not only does it look good as an end result but they also think it's a better way, a more basic way of doing it?

Well, there are people who enjoy watching the horses work. But for the most part, it's strictly from the standpoint of a neater job with less damage to their property.

That's a change in values right there.

Definitely. And, you know, a forest is no different from your garden. There comes a time when the stuff has to be harvested. Or it's going to blow down or crowd out the young stuff so that it doesn't grow. Of course, a lot of these skidder operations, they'll buy a lot, cut everything, clear-cut it, and then there's nothing left for a crow to land in. There'll never be lumber in there again. But what we do is that just about all our work is selective cutting. We just take out the trees that are going by and need to be taken out so that the others can grow.

How long does it take ordinarily to cut, for example, an acre?

There again, it makes a difference how far you have to haul the stuff to get it to a truck. Also how thick the lumber is. You may have an acre with only about 1,500 feet of logs or you might have an acre with 20,000 feet of logs on it. The acreage doesn't matter so much as how thick the stand is on it, or whether it's nice tall stuff or whether it's one and two log trees. It makes a difference.

———————

Bob excuses himself to answer the phone. He talks about a clearing job and the spring mud season he has to contend with—cold at night, warm during the day. He says into the phone that yesterday in the woods the ground had only 2 inches of slop, but it was still frozen hard underneath. The temperature dropped to 22 degrees last night. Not bad enough to stop work.

He has four horses, although he says he shouldn't. He buys and sells them. Just seems he can't stick to two at a time, which are all he really needs. In fact, he sold one this week, took an old mare in trade. He's going back to New Holland, Pennsylvania, Amish country, for another auction, and he's probably going to sell two and buy one or two while he's there.

Amish country is horse country. Special draft horse auctions are held in the first four months of the year. Sometimes up to 400 head are up for sale. The work horses come in from all over the country and that's where he picks up his own.

———————

What kind of horses do you use?

Belgians. I've had a Percheron or two, but I prefer the Belgians. And I prefer to train them myself. The horses I've had that are already trained are not quite trained the way that I want, is the best way to put it. I want them so that they'll mind when they're spoken to, and I want them to know what I'm saying. Some horses are inclined to be rather bullheaded. I suppose more or less like people.

You find that the Belgians work the best for you?

The thing I like about Belgians is that they have much better feet and legs on them. Percherons' feet aren't nearly as good. They're apt to be more brittle and crack. Percherons always have black feet. Horses with black feet are not good!

Do Belgians and Percherons have the same strength more or less?

It's six of one, half a dozen the other. Again, it's like men; they're all different. One horse may weigh 1,600 and be strong and another may weigh the same and be half again as strong.

Of course, we pull horses, too, at county fairs. A lot of people say you can't work horses in the woods and pull them, too, at fairs. You go into the woods and you get killed with them. But that isn't so. We use them right.

. . . I prefer the Belgians. And I prefer to train them myself. . . . I want them so that they'll mind when they're spoken to, and I want them to know what I'm saying.

What are the dangers of using horses in the woods?

Of course, no matter whether you use horses or tractors, woods are dangerous. You can get hurt easily in the woods. Well, for instance, if a horse doesn't mind and you're trying to hook a chain and he decides to leave and he just jumps ahead, he could cut your hand off in the chain. Or the carts you use can tip over if they get caught on something. That's why I say first off you want a horse that minds in the woods; it's got to mind. If it doesn't, you've got your life right in your hands.

Can you tell right away whether it's going to be a good working horse for you?

I don't have to work him an hour and I know whether I want him or not.

What's the first clue? He just doesn't mind?

That's the thing. He's just bullheaded. You try to back him
up two steps and he jumps ahead three. I've seen horses where
there's room enough to turn around if the horse is sensible, but
you half turn around and he sours and jumps into a brush pile.
It's just that he wasn't trained right to begin with, he wasn't broke
properly. If the horse has got any smarts and they're broke right
and pay attention, they do about what you ask them.

Have you found one that understands English yet?

I've found some that don't understand anything! They're all
kinds. There's an old saying that no horse was ever born balky,
but a lot of people make them balky while they're breaking them.
They get them so fouled up that you can't ever straighten them
out.

How long does it take you to train a horse?

There again, it varies with the horse. I just bought a pair of
horses a couple weeks ago, both broke supposedly. I'm sure that
they never had shoes on. The one horse fought all the way, really
bad. We had to rope her and throw her and everything else. It
never did give up. The other horse we had to rope, too. We roped
two feet on him. He got the idea by the time we were going for
the third foot. He was all right. We went ahead and shod him, but
he was a horse with some intelligence, he had some smarts. By the
time we got in the woods they were still the same way. He knew
something, she didn't.

Can you tell if they prefer working in different seasons?

It's a little hard to tell that. But in some horses you can tell
that they like to work. I've got one horse in the barn now that I've
had for three years and probably will have several more. In the
morning when you go down and after he's had his breakfast and
you're cleaning him off and harnessing him, he's just dying to get
in that truck and go to work. When he works, he just straight out
works, he's all business, Jerry is.

What's the difference in cost in clearing land with horses as opposed to skidders?

About the best way I could put it is that as far as pine stumpage, speaking in generalities, 45 to 50 dollars per 1,000 standing, depending on the quality of the pine, whereas skidders are probably paying 75 to 80 dollars for pine. They pay almost double what I do. As far as the landowner, he gets perhaps twice as much for his logs, but when they get done the owner hasn't much left but a field.

His 20-year-old son Rod worked with him last year but he got discouraged with the deep snow. They were doing a job up in East Washington and, of course, he says, that's the pits up there. Lots of granite boulders and steep hills. About the middle of December the snow was so deep that the horses couldn't get their feet up under their neck yokes. They had to quit. Then they cleared a lot over at West Deering, but it was rough there, too.

His son said to hell with this logging and went west. He joined Bob's married daughter and her husband outside Las Vegas, Nevada, to run equipment mining gold and silver. Who knows? Rod will probably be back in New England sometime.

What's the biggest area you ever cleared?

Well, I guess about 250 acres we did on one job. Of course, we had to bulldoze roads through so that the trucks could get back into the woods. Being that large, it would be just too unwieldly to haul out to the nearest highway. I've got a lot over in Jaffrey that I expect we'll do this summer. It's about 160 acres.

Are there other people around here that do the same work as you?

Not with horses too much. There really aren't too many of them today. Nobody wants to work that hard. It's easier just to shut the key off at night, go home, and forget it. With horses you still got a couple hours left brushing and grooming them, feeding them. They get feed three times a day.

You'd much rather do that than change the oil and put gas in.

Oh, yeah, much rather. I'm always up early in the morning so it doesn't bother me to go down and feed them at four-thirty or quarter to five. Oh, these other guys, all they want to do is just get on a tractor, turn the key, and off they go.

At eight o'clock.

Right.

Have you always worked hard at those hours? As a kid?

Yeah, I was raised on a dairy farm. Always got up early. It's not a big deal. Of course, I always go to bed fairly early at night. I don't sit up and watch TV half the night.

Well, there has been a big switch in work values.

Oh, definitely. There's all this talk about no work now, just can't find jobs. The ones that want to work are working. The ones that aren't working can't find jobs. There are plenty of jobs right in this area. They're just too damn lazy to work. They don't want to work, they just want to draw unemployment or welfare or whatever. I know a sawmill right down here. He's having an awful time with help. Two or three days ago he had a fella driving truck for him, hauling lumber and various things. So the other morning things were a little slow, so he asked him to do a little bit of manual labor for a couple hours. First thing he knew the guy was gone, he went home. He was too good to do manual labor. He was a truck driver, you know. They say jobs are scarce. If jobs are so scarce, I wouldn't care whether I was shoveling crap against the tide, if I got an hour's pay I'd be getting it. It's just a case of not wanting to work, that's just what it amounts to.

BOB SPECKMAN   121

Do you think it's a problem with the young people themselves?

Yes, it is. I don't know what's going to become of the next generation to follow this one because this one is bad. I guess it's going to be robots or computers or whatever.

What have you learned from your work over the years?

Well, basically, I guess it's a lot of knowledge of forestry. How to improve a forest, knowledge of what a 1,000 feet of lumber is, more or less walk through a lot and get a pretty good estimation of what's there. There's a lot over here I went through. We spent about three hours, it was about 42 acres. He asked me how much lumber I thought it was. I said, Well, I'm going to say roughly 20,000 feet of oak and 100,000 feet of pine. And the oak is going to come right on the money and the pine isn't going to be off too much, maybe over 100,000. After you spent a lot of years in the woods you can get a pretty good idea of what's there.

That's a satisfying skill to have learned.

Yes, it is, that you're pretty accurate of what you see.

Not many people hate trees, but here in New Hampshire you could take half the trees out and you wouldn't know the difference.

Ever since I was a kid, I remember people saying, God, the way they're cutting lumber, there won't be a tree left in this state. Do you know this lumber is growing faster than they're cutting? If a lot is selectively cut, it'll grow faster than it's taken out.

And it'll grow better.

Oh, definitely.

Now what does it mean exactly when a lot is cut selectively?

Well, it means you go into a clump of trees and you pick, number one, the largest trees before they go the other way.

Number two, any tree grows and crotches out into two branches. That'll never be a nice tree, it's just a double-stem tree. You take those kinds of trees out and leave the nice tall straight trees that are growing. You can almost see them growing after that. They're more efficient, they get the sunlight, they just really shoot up. This lot we're doing over here should really have been cut 30, 40 years ago. The trees are getting red rot in the center in a big share of them. They're real old trees; they're just standing still, that's what it amounts to. You can count the rings on a stump of a tree, and you can tell how old it is; it grows one ring each year. These rings on those trees over there are so tight it's impossible to count them. So it's just not growing, it's right at a standstill for years.

They're not doing anybody any good.

Right. They're starting to die from the bottom up. When you fall a tree, in the center of the stump they'll be a rot in the round. So it won't be too many more years before it'll be lost. As I said, it's just like your garden.

We go outside and walk down a slight incline to the barn Bob built. It's a sturdy, efficient structure that matches the huge horses inside. A Percheron he has weighs about 1,800 pounds. The horse stamps and snorts and smashes against the railings. Another minute of this and the whole barn will collapse. The ruckus is nothing to sneeze at, that's for sure. Even-natured Bob adjusts a confining railing and quiets the horse.

"He's a pretty good horse," he says. "He's half man-shy. He's a little bit scared of you and if he's given the chance he'll scare you, too."

One wall of the barn is covered with harnesses. He says it seems every time he gets a new strap the price has gone up another 20 percent. Expensive items. You have to keep them oiled and taken care of.

For his work he needs not too much else—a chain saw, shoeing equipment, a scoot, sometimes a log cart with two wheels, a truck to haul the horses.

He takes Jerry, the hardworking gentleman horse, outside for a picture. Jerry stands about 17 hands high, big and husky. Friendly, too. Then back inside he goes, and Bob talks of shoeing draft horses. He's pretty much always done it himself. He learned when he was a teenager. His back isn't what it used to be these days so he has to hire somebody once in a while to shoe. Not too many men around nowadays know how to shoe a draft horse. "They're afraid of these big horses," he says. "They want these little saddle horses."

Only once was he kicked. He was about 17 or 18. Got kicked in the face and broke his nose. He knocks on wood.

———————————

You have to be alert out there in the woods and around horses, keep your wits about you.

Oh, yes, you got to be awake all the time. It only takes a second to goof up.

Would you like to see more people clear land with horses?

Definitely. I'd like to see the land taken care of more than it has been with the skidders. Of course, today everything's mass production—wham, bam, in and out.

You're a rarity.

A diehard, I guess.

CLEARING LAND WITH HORSES

Margaret MacArthur

Folk Singing

Margaret MacArthur

Marlboro, Vermont

Born in Chicago, Margaret MacArthur in her early life traveled throughout the country before settling in Missouri. It was always backcountry roads and simple living, and then more traveling. At 16, she entered the University of Chicago and there met John, her husband. They moved to Vermont in 1948 and bought their present house in 1951.

She started singing as a child. Her mother taught her nursery rhymes and her stepfather cowboy songs. As a teenager she learned the longer ballads, which now she is most fond of singing. When she settled for good in Vermont, she looked for New England songs and collected some from older people in the area. "It was word-of-mouth contact," she says.

Their farmhouse was built in 1803 high on one of the sloping edges of the long Green Mountains. The original beams of the snug house still show in the country living room. A wood stove waits in the center. Antique string instruments—zithers, mandolins, fiddles—hang on two walls, rows of books fill the opposite wall. These instruments and books show a thoughtfulness about her, the way she stops to think before answering questions. A certain gentleness also is evident in her manner as well as in her songs and the soft folk instruments she plays—the dulcimer, harp-zither, guitar.

At the same time, country living is often far from gentle. Fields to tend, wood to cut, snow to shovel. Just before sitting down to talk, Margaret has been harvesting the garden. John (a physicist teaching at nearby Marlboro College) walks in with a huge bucket of yellow snap beans, offers the whole bucket (an obvious ploy so he won't have to snap them), and then goes to the wood-wall kitchen overlooking four horses in a rejuvenated apple orchard. The rest of Vermont stretches northward. Now and then Margaret calls back to John to verify a recollection.

You must have been asked this a hundred times, but what makes a good folk song?

I think a folk song either tells a good story or sometimes gives a feel of life, of how people live. In general, I think of a folk song as pretty old, but there are songs that are being written now.

Are they connected always with a social situation, or do they give us a political message of some sort?

I don't sing political songs. I like them, but I've been unable to present them myself very easily. What people would be singing in 1808, for instance, might be described as what we call parlor songs. You'd really have to search historically very hard to find political songs.

Were old-time folk songs written down?

Well, it's said that before people could read or write the songs were passed on by word of mouth. Some of the old-time Vermonters kept notebooks and jotted songs down just as we would today. Mr. Fred Atwood of Dover, from whom I learned a lot of songs, had composition books that he had had as a boy. Through his lifetime he wrote them down.

With the notes, too?

No, just the lyrics. No, I've never collected songs from anybody who could write the music. They sang them for me. They just wrote down the words to keep the poetry in them in mind, but they remembered the tunes. And they remembered the songs, too. Not everybody from whom I collected them had written down the words. Mr. Atwood learned a lot from his father.

That must have been a treasure find.

Yes. That was in 1961.

Those songs must have gone back quite a time if they were from his father.

And his grandfather. His father had learned some of them from his grandfather. Some of them probably had been brought from England from the first of that family. It's kind of historic and you feel that you're linked to some far past. Some of the songs he sang were about England and some were about Vermont. He'd written one or two himself.

Mr. Atwood was a very backwoods type of person. He had moved to Connecticut when he was a young man and had spent the rest of his life down there. I found out about him and invited him up here. He came up and he sang for us here at the house and stayed with us a couple of days. Of all the people I'd met in Vermont, he gave me more songs than anyone else.

In a sense, are you part of the continuum of these folk songs?

Yes, I guess so, although I've recorded songs, and instead of word of mouth they're on record. My kids have learned songs. Megan, Dan, and Gary play with me. In this way, it is a sort of continuum. I've sung these songs, and now they're singing the songs.

Does a recording eliminate the possibility of passing on the folk songs through word of mouth?

I don't think so, because a lot of people have learned songs from my records; people who wouldn't have had access to me have had access to my records.

Margaret sang as a performer in college, but her first paying job was down the mountainside to Brattleboro at radio station WTSA.

Her reputation grew, and when she made the record "Folk Songs in Vermont" for Folkways, she was brought into wider circulation.

With five children, she limited her performances. Her grown children, like their mother, live self-sufficient lives. Four of them live in separate houses they built on the family farm; the oldest son lives in Taos, New Mexico.

Margaret's own parents moved to Kentucky about the time she moved to Vermont. She visits them often and is known as a New England folk singer who collects Kentucky songs, too.

She's known as well for a special old-time instrument. This small cross-strung harp-zither was given to her by Merle Landman of Rawsonville, Vermont, and John restored it. The instrument was made probably in 1905 or so and had been hanging in Landman's barn. It turns out that an instrument maker in the Adirondacks started making copies of it and calls it the MacArthur harp. Others in Ohio and Kentucky are making them as well. The MacArthur harp is spreading out over the back countryside.

John made her a cherry-wood dulcimer in 1961 that she's been playing ever since. She takes it and the harp-zither outside and sits against a maple beside the rock garden she and John assembled. The garden is a beauty, all sorts of delicate flowers interlaced through steps of gray granite slabs. It fits Margaret and it fits her music.

If you had your way totally, what would be the most supreme way of singing? What setting, what situation?

Say in an old church, which is where I sang Sunday in Rockingham, Vermont. I sang in this beautiful Rockingham meeting house, this antique church. I like to sing in historic places, historical houses, historic churches, old buildings, because the songs I sing fit right in. It's an unamplified situation. You don't need speakers kicking around. And I also like to sing just in the living room.

When guests come in?

Sometimes. Although that's what we used to do all the time, it's almost harder now. Sometimes people *expect* us—"this *artist*"—

and here we're just kicking around the house. But for years I just sang the songs for fun and it's been quite rewarding for me to realize that some people are interested in the songs and want to hear them.

Around New England has the crowd interested in folk songs been about the same size over the years?

Well, people around here know me now and more people will turn out to hear me, not because of a new interest in folk songs. It wouldn't be the same in Boston, for instance. The same number of people came to hear me in Boston in 1960 when I used to play at the Club 47. I really don't know whether the people come to hear me or want to hear the music. It's hard to tell.

What about the songs? What are the ones you like especially, even though the audience may not like them as much?

I love the ancient ballads like "Barbara Allen" and "Matthew Groves," "King John and the Bishop of Canterbury," and the "Weeping Willow Tree." These are classic ballads of the English language. I do love them very much. They paint a real picture in my mind and in anybody's mind who sits and listens to them, too. You can see why they've lived so long. They're good stories. Well, "Barbara Allen" isn't such a good story, but there are some beautiful lines in it.

But I also like songs that give a flavor of life at some point or another. I made a record of some New England farm songs which are quite dear to my heart. The songs are about different things that happen on a farm at different times of the year, like maple sugaring and the plowing and spinning and weaving and harvesting. They're old-time songs. I wrote one song on the record after hearing an old story, so it's a versification of a folk tale set to music. I made the verse and I wrote the music, but I didn't make up the story.

In a way, do you sing the songs to have an influence?

No.

But you've had an influence. You speak of your children and what they are doing by living simply and being as self-sufficient as they can be, building simple direct housing for others. It's a sort of ripple effect from you, although maybe not from the songs as such.

I don't think that's ever been a motive. But we influenced our children just by example, I think.

Were your parents living somewhat the way you're living now?

Yes. My stepfather is a forester and we lived in a lot of primitive places where I was growing up without electricity, very backwards places, every place was really far from town and extremely far from any city. Two of our sons have no electricity in their houses, and we all raise our own vegetables.

When you sing, is there something special that you'd like to convey to the audience in some way?

I like to convey to the audience that I'm really interested in and have respect for the poetry. It's not just *music* that you sit and listen to. You can, but if you can get yourself into the story or imagine that it's happening to you, it's better. It's like a play; you have to imagine who's talking. The characterization keeps changing. If I'm singing for young people, say 12-year-olds, I do talk about that. They're able to do that, but they're all so television-oriented now that I have a fear that if I didn't explain to them how to listen to this song—for instance, he says something and another person says something and you have to keep track of who's saying what—then the song will just go by them. Adults can usually do it because they weren't raised by television—or some of them would. I have a real fear that people are going to lose that ability—to read a book. They won't know what's going on, they won't be able to imagine what's happening; that it's just going to be a bunch of words. I'm scared about that. People see so much television and you know who's talking because you can see who's talking. But what if you can't see who's talking and you can't imagine who's talking or what's happening?

132

I like to convey to the audience that I'm really interested in and have respect for the poetry. It's not just music that you sit and listen to. You can, but if you can get yourself into the story or imagine that it's happening to you, it's better.

MARGARET MACARTHUR   133

There's an alarming statistic that says the average number of hours a television set is on in an average household in the United States is seven hours and two minutes every day. Are you a storyteller who sings?

Well, maybe. Songs are stories. So maybe there is a resurgence in the ballad to go along with the resurgence of interest in the story, but you don't dramatize in the ballad, you don't emote. You just present the words. People are supposed to color it up themselves in their own minds. Storytelling is different, perhaps allowing for more dramatization.

What is the core of New England you're singing about as opposed to some other region of the country?

Well, I live here and I do a lot with the land—between us and our kids. It just seems to be historically related to the way I live, these old songs. One of the songs was a ballad from England. She says she can do more work, he says he can do more work in a day than she could do in three. She counters by saying we'll trade. She goes out and plows the field and he fouls up everything. Maybe it's all related to the way we live here in this old house which we keep in some kind of flavor of the way the old house always was. So we feel connected to the people who built the house in 1803. I like to have this relationship, too, with the songs, feel back through the songs to the person who made up the song in the first place.

Through all these songs of Vermont and New England, the land, the farm, the old characters back in history, have you seen some patterns of values that have been emphasized?

No, I don't think values are included in the songs, very rarely. Well, there's a song of what on earth is the world coming to since things have changed 50 years ago; man is always tampering with nature's wondrous laws. I suppose that has some. It's saying that life was better 50 years ago because life moved more slowly. But it wasn't 50 years ago now; it was 50 years ago when people had fast horses; 50 years before that they had oxen instead. So it was the good old days. There's a lot of danger in talking about the good old days. They could have been very much

FOLK SINGING

worse. It says in that song that the children did a half-day's work before they went to school.

But you sing these old songs, so they must have something in them that appeals to you more than the contemporary songs, and if it's not the values that they express, then what would that be, do you think?

Well, I don't live in a contemporary way. Maybe that does have something to do with values. I don't think it's a nostalgic thing with me because we have really been able to live in an earlier way. Our children have done the same.

So are you saying . . . ?

. . . turning my back on the present-day U.S.A.? Probably.

Or you're living in the time of some of the songs you're singing, or you prefer that time, at least?

I can't do that either, can't really say that. The songs are simple, they're really not complicated, and I wish life were simple and not complicated. Maybe there is some nostalgia in there. I don't know if it's nostalgia or stubbornness. The songs we sing probably reflect that. Other people sing the same kind of songs, but they live in apartments in the city. There isn't any way that an audience in a big festival can tell the difference, but it makes me feel good to present the songs that are related in one way or another to the life I lead.

The lyrics printed here are from one of the few songs that Margaret has written herself. Like the ballads of old she likes to sing, her own song grew from a living legend and a living love story. This true story goes like this:

In 1974 Bert Salva and Mary Shiminski had a quarrel in Long Island. She didn't want to see him ever again and, in fact, traveled with her family north to Vermont on vacation for three weeks. Salva followed her in his big tractor-trailer truck. Wherever Mary went, Salva was sure to follow.

Mary wouldn't see or talk to him. One day the family drove under the railroad trestle and over the bridge across the Connecticut River to New Hampshire for a stay at Spofford Lake. Hiding sign of himself, Salva left his tractor-trailer and walked 30 miles from Putney, Vermont, to the lake. He begged Mary Shiminski for a ride back; she refused and showed him dust.

Back in Brattleboro, he bought $25 worth of black and white spray paint. That night from 11 P.M. he hung from one hand down the side of the trestle. For hours he sprayed the huge iron trestle black to block out the graffiti. Then, working until 5:30 A.M., he sprayed the immortal words in white: "Mary Shiminski I Love You!"

The next morning Mary and her family ate breakfast at the Howard Johnson's restaurant beside the overpass and saw the world-wide proclamation of love (later the highway department estimated 2 million people saw the message). Mary Shiminski was embarrassed and angry enough to ask two police officers what to do. They offered her a cup of coffee and said she should be honored.

Mary returned to Long Island. So did Salva. Mary kept slamming the door in his face, changing her telephone number, siccing her guard dog after love-sick Salva. Salva kept knocking and calling and feeding the dog Kentucky Fried Chicken. By August 7, 1974, Mary Shiminski just couldn't hold out any longer. She and Salva drove to South Carolina, got married, moved to Riverside, California, and now have two children and a well-fed guard dog.

Mary Shiminski I Love You

By Margaret MacArthur

There's a railroad bridge by the river
Where old 5 crosses Route 9.
Six hours it took me to write these words,
I'll tell you they were on my mind;

When I wrote:
(*chorus*)
"Mary Shiminski, I love you"
Oh, Lord, what was I doing?
Hanging by one hand from the railroad bridge
Writing by the light of the moon.

Mary left me in New Jersey,
She went to a small Vermont town.

I hitched up my rig, my big tractor-trailer
And I headed north to claim my own.

I found Mary in Putney
But when I knocked at her door
She sicced her old dog on me and he tore my pants.
I cursed and I hollered and I swore. But I wrote:
  (chorus)

Mary she went on a picnic.
I hiked in fifteen miles or more
But when I arrived, she left with a friend.
My heart and my feet were sore.
  (no chorus)

Mary she called the sheriff.
She gave that man my name;
He said, "Take your rig, that big tractor-trailer
And go back in from where you came."
  (no chorus)

So I'll go back to New Jersey,
No comfort here can I find
But before I go, I'll write these words
To the meanest of all woman kind. I'll write:
  (chorus)

Mary came down to Ho Jo's,
Where old 5 crosses Route 9.
She saw these words on the railroad bridge
And her heart commenced a cryin'.

Mary called down to New Jersey.
Said, "My love, married we'll be."
So he hitched up his rig, his big tractor-trailer,
And headed for the north country.
  (no chorus)

These lovers got married,
They have little ones one, two, three;
Through good times and bad, that old railroad bridge
Lives in their memory. Where he wrote:
  (chorus)
  (what was *he* doin')

MARGARET MACARTHUR   137

RUSSELL PIERCE

Wool Milling

Russell Pierce

Bartlettyarns, Harmony, Maine

Since 1821, high in interior Maine, Bartlettyarns has been taking in raw wool and spinning it into yarns. The process is more complicated than this, as Russell Pierce, current owner, explains, but the values, attitudes, and relationships between wool grower and miller are still pretty much the same.

With its fascinating, tried-and-true nineteenth-century machines, the mill is located on the south side of Harmony, a village set in the corrugated farm and woodlands of central Maine. Ozias Bartlett founded the first mill and it remained in the Bartlett family in the traditional New England way until 1947. In the early days farmers always had sheep and plenty of pasture land. They brought their raw wool to the mill to be carded and spun, and they received knitting yarn in return. (Farmers still do that today.) Then during the winter the women knitted sweaters, mittens, caps, socks. For the mill, the colder the fall the better the yarn sale. Warm Novembers meant hard times.

Pierce is a tall, slim, easy-going man who speaks slowly and clearly all the way to the end of his sentences. He enjoys what he's doing and talking about how it's possible in our modern hard-nosed money world to run a business with a sense of neighborhood still in mind.

Evidently, the mill was first designed to serve the needs of the immediate townspeople.

The original family was interested basically in weaving yarns and weaving fabrics, cloth, for people who were raising sheep in the area. Within a very few years they stopped manufacturing cloth and specialized in yarn making. Over the years they made blanket material and other kinds of material from time to time, but essentially this has been a yarn-spinning outfit. It operates similar to what I used to hear as a kid—the village miller who grinds up somebody's wheat to make flour. Taking in wool from people raising sheep and returning it as yarn. This technically is called custom spinning or custom processing. We still do that; it's the backbone of the business—custom work. Most people nowadays don't get their own wool back because we're at the point now where we have to make commercially economical lot sizes.

In the early days were the flocks large?

Somewhere I read there were over a half million sheep in New England. Today there are under 50,000. Maine was a large sheep-growing area. New England is a sheep-growing area, northern New England particularly. There's very little flat land suitable for large farms, so raising dairy cattle or sheep is ideal.

Around here you don't see a large 1,000-acre corn field, unless it's very undulating, but you can pasture sheep on rough pastures. For a variety of reasons, sheep raising has dropped off in New England. In recent years the sheep population has started to grow again because more people are leaving the city and going back to the country, back to the earth, so they'll raise a few sheep, primarily for their own meat purposes. Then they have this wool left over. We're one of the few places where they can take their wool and have it converted into an end product or trade it for an end product.

What accounted for the decline of the sheep-raising industry here? What were the main factors?

Well, as the country grew and people developed the West, they found that it was more efficient to raise larger herds on huge tracts of land. What I think it boiled down to is that New England became industrialized. People moved off the farm to work in the cities to make shoes and work in the textile mills. Also, I think a lot of the wool that was used in the New England mills was coming in from South Africa, England, Australia, and New Zealand. It began to be cheaper to import raw material.

Wasn't there a migration of labor to the South, too?

That started really after World War II. The textile companies started being run by people conscious of half a cent differential. A lot of these mills used cotton as a raw material. So they just moved the mills closer to the source of either the supply of cheap cotton or cheap labor. Those battles are still being fought by companies like J. P. Stevens today. But for some reason Bartlettyarns has survived all of this ebb and flow, essentially because it has been servicing neighbors. Now our neighborhood is all 50 states and Canada, but it's still a neighborhood. Sheep growers in the vicinity of Harmony still bring their wool here. People who come in here tell me that their grandparents brought their wool here. We get to know a grandfather who will bring in his granddaughter. I found out the other day that a granddaughter is a prizewinner from some of the fleeces she's raised. He was very proud of the blue ribbon she'd won in Vermont. So there's just this basic neighborly friendliness.

Then there's some sort of continuing link from generation to generation.

That's right. And it seems to have continued regardless of who's operated the Bartletts. There's a heritage here, a character if you will, to the business that could be disrupted very, very easily with a change in the approach to running the business, a change by a new owner. It's just whether you want to run your business in a very hard-nosed, profit-oriented way, which could easily say let's move this mill to the South, or to continue running it as a service to people, as a business everybody enjoys being involved with.

Another reason that Bartlettyarns has survived is that the company has stayed pretty much tied to the wool as opposed to any of the man-made fibers. The mills that have gone to the man-made fibers found that they have to keep up with technological developments in order to remain competitive. Wool mills that are spinning on a system called worster, as opposed to the woolen system that we use, also have to keep up with technology, to a lesser degree. You'll see that our equipment is relatively primitive and this has benefits. We have found a niche where the product is demanded and accepted by our customers and we've also found a niche that no larger company seems interested in because there's not much glamor. There's not the opportunity of pushing a button in the morning, having a digital read-out every five minutes of what's happening, having a mill so clean that you can eat off the floor, and at the end of the afternoon the freight cars are automatically loaded for you. Now that type of mill can be put up anywhere in the world. But that's really the difference that Bartlettyarns has survived. It's stayed simple. All the old phrases— "We've tended to our knitting."

This is one of the oldest mills in the country run the way you run it.

Yes, I would say that in making yarn there are probably three or four mills in the United States that will take in wool in exchange for yarn or will do custom spinning.

This is a very basic way of dealing with business in our nanosecond computer age. How do these values continue to flourish? Is this an aberration of the 1980s?

I think it is. We have people who come in here from communities along the coast of Maine who have all the preppie colors on. Let's put it this way, we have people who come in here who are obviously very well-to-do. I haven't seen any Gucci loafers here, but we've come close to it. For some reason or another, they have some sheep. They like sheep. It may be a hobby flock, maybe they have a house in the country and it's a way to mow their lawn. Obviously, they are not interested in getting the yarns, in getting rid of the wool. We have other people who come in here who obviously are making their living from sheep and that's the other end of the spectrum, I guess. They will take their sheep hides to a tanner, they'll bring the wool to use for yarn, they will have their meat slaughtered and sold to Greek butchers. They are very knowledgeable about sheep husbandry. They know all about pasturage, about feeding practices, lambing practices. They are people who have closed-circuit TV in lambing season so they can see and assist the animal on a cold winter's night. They keep careful records, the weight of the offspring, the growth of the animal, crossbreeding. They are professional people.

Except for the closed-circuit television, this could very well be done the way it has been done for generations?

That's true.

Are you viewing this mill as a way of continuing long-entrenched values of New England?

Well, a lot of people arrive here with New England license plates and they are not New Englanders! There are many people outside New England who are attracted to us because they see us as, like the title of your book, basic Yankee. Yes, it's a basic Yankee way of doing things. A little barter never hurt anybody and this appeals to people. But this is not really barter. Wool is brought to us and a value is put on it, so this isn't a tax dodge or the underground economy. It's a straightforward business transaction.

The original mill burned down about 1922, but Harry Bartlett in the true sturdy New England way built another one right away on the same spot, the west side of Higgins Stream. In fact, he drove by horse and sleigh to North Dexter to rent an available mill in the meantime. There in the middle of a Maine winter he kept the manufacture of Bartlettyarns going until he could move into his new mill.

Pierce needs to process lots of about 1,000 pounds of raw wool. To put it into perspective, the average sheep produces a fleece of between 8 to 12 pounds, depending on the breed. Some breeds are heavier on the wool side and less on the meat side, and vice versa. Today a sheep farmer can get a Bartlettyarns blanket for $24 and 16 pounds of wool.

Curiously, the sleek modern one-word "Bartlettyarns" has been used for the company since the early 1920s. A basic business can still have a streamlined logo.

During all those long early years there wasn't the challenge that acrylic has given wool. Does that spell doom for your business?

No, on the contrary, because people recognize the value of 100 percent natural fibers, like wool, silk, or cotton. If you go to Barney's in New York and still pay 500 dollars for a business suit, you're going to want to have something that's going to last more than two seasons. People perceive that 100 percent wool will last them much longer. And everybody has a 100 percent wool sweater.

There's a fashion trend, and there's this trend that started in the sixties with the greening of America and the return to the earth. There's a lot of that going on in New England, but there's a lot of that also underlying the values of what you would say is "Midwestern." Rather than wearing a flashy polyester doubleknit suit, they still stick to the old wool sportjacket. I don't think those values are easily changed. People can go to fads, but they come back to basics.

Are you sticking with wool all the way, or would you move into another natural fiber such as cotton?

No, wool. It sounds like the guy who makes buggy whips and that's all he's going to make. Ever since a kid you hear you've got to diversify. Not so. If we started making cotton or acrylics or anything other than wool, we would start losing our hard-core customers who depend upon us as experts in the field. We have to send our wool out to custom dye houses and some of our yarns are dyed in the skein after they've been spun. We've had one dye house send back our skeins tied with acrylic something. It just jarred everybody, just to have a little 6-inch piece of acrylic on it! It just didn't fit. So we cut it and threw it away, but you always worry if a little piece of that fiber sticks to that skein. What happens if a customer comes across something that looks shiny and silvery? It bothers us.

————

Pierce's office is a crowded desk and telephone in an old wood building directly across the road from the metal-sided mill. He shares the office with a secretary and bookkeeper. After talking awhile here,

WOOL MILLING

he gives "the tour" and we start down the half-dozen indoor wooden steps to an adjoining room with a low-slung ceiling and stacks of grain sacks stuffed with raw and processed wool.

Much of any woolen mill business rests on the 80/20 rule—"80 percent sweaters, 20 percent everything else"—he says. It's a sweater business basically and after that it's leg warmers, caps, mittens.

Today some clever machines can put someone into business by working from a kitchen table. This home industry comes from machine knitters that can be operated with a punch card for certain patterns. As Pierce explains, put a motor on it, set it on a dining room table, and you have an electronic sweater maker for about a $500 investment. If you have an outlet for the sweaters, you can make $400 a week.

Before going to the mill across the road, we walk into the barn-storage room. Here's where the growers back up their farm trucks and swing sacks of newly sheared spring wool onto the platform. The wool feels sticky because it's full of natural lanolin.

The first step must be to clean the wool as it comes in.

Yes, we wash our wool with a process called scouring. You can either scour with a sulfuric acid solution that will burn out all the vegetable matter, burrs and what-not, but it also eliminates the lanolin. We want to leave the lanolin in the wool because we're selling a fisherman yarn, so-called because it has some weather resistance created by leaving some lanolin in the wool. Lanolin left in the wool makes it easier to spin and it also develops a weather resistance.

What percentage of lanolin is left in?

Well under 10 percent. It's a trade secret. So because we leave lanolin in, we use a straight mild detergent scouring job and that results in some of this field chaff being left in the wool. We clean out virtually 100 percent of the chaff in the spinning of the yarn, but you'll find in the yarn, particularly those that have nothing but the natural wool in them, that there'll be a little piece of grass or chaff still in the yarn. I always kid and say that we leave that in to make it authentic, but it is a mark of 100 percent wool to find those specks, unless you're buying a worsted yarn in which case it would have all been removed by the acid bath.

So the actual spinning process begins downstairs here.

Yes. This white wool is typical of that brought to us. It has a nice softness and some of the field matter in it because of the way we scour. Generally, the way we tell is by grabbing a handful and just start pulling. It has a lot of strength and yet some softness to it. That will make good yarn. As I start pulling on this, too, it starts fluffing up and that's another attribute that we're looking for.

What about this lightish gray color?

That's coming from an older animal. Depending upon the parentage, say a black ram and a white ewe, it might produce a black lamb. As that lamb grows older it will tend to whiten out, gray out.

And this machine?

This is where we mix our color. They're first mixed in this machine, which is called a picker. The patent on this machine is 1879 and the age of the machine is probably the early 1900s. However, I have seen this identical model in a very modern woolen mill, three of them, as a matter of fact. It does its job very well and has not been modernized. The inside of the machine is composed of several conveyors made out of wooden slats. One has sharp little pins on it and as the wool goes up the conveyor, being carried up by the pins, it's then combed off the pins by this bar with the large teeth. So the wool tends to tumble around in here before it can escape and go over the top. In doing that the wool is teased or opened up. In this tumbling we can also add the color, so in effect it's like a mixing bowl. All of these colors we make against a basic recipe or formula. We'll make a 400-pound cake— so many pounds of the white wool, so many pounds of the color

WOOL MILLING

This white wool is typical of that brought to us. . . . It has a lot of strength and yet some softness to it. That will make good yarn.

wool, depending on what we're trying to do.

Then the wool goes into this other machine, the duster, and spins around like a centrifuge pattern. This way the chaff or field matter gets spun out of the wool. It's what you find in a vacuum cleaner.

We now have to blow the wool upstairs. It's been prepared, opened, dusted, and blended.

Now what color is this going to be?

This lot going through here is called Light Feather. It has five colors in it. Primarily, it's white wool with little flecks of blue, gold, red, and lilac and it makes a really beautiful yarn. Now the purpose of this card is to comb the fibers of the wool so that instead of going every which way, they lie parallel with each other. When they start to lie parallel, you can spin them into yarn very easily.

The wool is then weighed with this little hand balance and drops onto a feed table that starts its way through the card machine. The card is a machine that really hasn't changed in design for a long time, a hundred years or more. This one dates back to 1919. It's a series of cylinders wrapped with belting material that has very fine needle-like wire that protrudes out of a belt. There's a large cylinder and wool is basically traveling around the cylinder. It is worked off the cylinder with these medium-size rollers. The wool is stripped from the medium-size rollers and redeposited onto the big cylinder. As the fibers begin to run parallel to each other they form a web. They begin to look like a paper mill.

Now the wool is taken off the large cylinder onto this medium-size cylinder. It goes onto a meticulously machined, stainless-steel roller, much like a ringer on an old-fashioned washing machine.

At the end of this machine it's being divided into strands small enough in width so that we can spin it. That is accomplished by running it through a series of rollers that have grooves in them. They actually slice up the web. So now we have narrow strips of wool coming out of the machine. They enter this final part of the machine called a condenser where they are rubbed between these green-aproned rolls. So now the wool has been divided into 100 ends. Four ends are waste so we're winding up 96 ends on four different spools, 24 per spool. They're rubbed up into a nice little piece of rope.

Now here's demonstration time. This is a piece of roping. If I pull it apart you can get an idea of the wool fibers. They have quite a bit of strength to them and a lot of crimp, which is typical of our wool in the northern hemisphere, particularly New England. It's that crimp that gives wool its softness and also gives it its strength. Because all you have to do is give that wool a little twist and, bingo, you've got yarn that's tough. It's certainly a characteristic of wool, but I know a sheep didn't tell anybody. Some very clever person in Europe, maybe in Palestine, who knows, learned that that was the trick. The twist.

The second floor of the mill clacks with two rows of busy machines. This is about as close to the old-time small New England woolen mill scene as you can get—dark wood floors and walls, intriguing machines performing precise speedy functions, natural raw materials at one end of the process and finely crafted finished products at the other. Twenty-four employees work in scattered areas at the mill.

On this floor, one row of machines prepares the wool for the other row. It's this second row that is mesmerizing. It's the mule. This machine, the only one of its kind left in New England and one of the very few left in the country, is a series of more than 200 spinning bobbins set on an axle of ten iron wheels. It spins about 50 to 70 pounds of yarn an hour. The mule stretches across the entire floor and rolls back and forth on the wheels set on tracks. A series of complex lever motions operate as the mule rolls back pulling thin strands of yarn to twist, spin, and roll. Then the mule rolls back toward the large supplying spools of waiting yarn for another series of functions.

All the while, a single attendant keeps a watchful eye. If a string breaks, he repairs it without stopping the mule. His motions are quick and delicate, swift flicks of his experienced hands and fingers. No knots are tied, just dextrous manual twists that use the natural adhesion of the natural wool. It's all very fascinating.

RUSSELL PIERCE

This is the famous mule.

Yes, a spinning mule and it is duplicating the motions that a person using a walking wheel, a spinning machine, would use. The old-fashioned spinning wheel required the spinner to spin the yarn and when that strand was spun to change the position of her hand so that the yarn would wind up on a bobbin much like you'd wind a piece of string on a yo-yo.

As the mule moves out toward us, it is bringing the unspun roping from the spool and that strand is being spun. The spinning process takes place as the roping slips off the tips of these bobbins. When the carriage mule retracts, a wire changes the angle of the yarn so that the spun yarn winds onto the bobbin as the mule retracts. That's the same thing as a hand spinner.

It was designed in the late 1770s. It was a cross between another type of spinning machine and the spinning jenny. Hence, the name of mule because it was a crossbreed. It turned out to be a revolutionary machine in the early 1800s in England. You can imagine this machine being tended by ten-year-old boys and girls. This machine is a relatively new one, probably one of the last to be made. It's a 1948 model, the Cadillac of mules. It was a very complex machine for the 1800s. Claims have been made that this was the most complicated machine in the early Industrial Revolution. It replaced 200 hand-spinners and created a consistency in yarn. This is doing exactly what a hand spinner would be doing if he had a consistent-size roping and could reach back 6 feet from that bobbin with a great big spinning wheel. So our yarns may be a little commercial, but in effect our yarns do have this home-spun quality to them.

As the mule moves out toward us, it is bringing the unspun roping from the spool and that strand is being spun. The spinning process takes place as the roping slips off the tips of these bobbins.

ADALYN DANIELS

Carving Apple-Head Dolls

Adalyn Daniels

Atkinson, New Hampshire

The bright-blossomed dogwood tree at the front of the house can't compete with Adalyn Daniels as she opens the door with her shining smile and greeting. She lives with her daughter Scottie who works as a receptionist for the *New Hampshire Times* in Concord. Adalyn doesn't look, act, or think her age. She's 92.

She's been making apple-head dolls for about 30 or 35 years. She can't remember exactly, and who cares. Born in Marlboro, Massachusetts, of a musical family (grandfather a musician, aunt a soprano, grandmother an artist), she herself is a sculptor. Her small statue of St. Francis and one of a mermaid stand in the entrance garden. Is she a New Englander? "Oh, yeah," she says, "dyed in the wool, way back. My folks came over on the *Mayflower*. Way back."

She leads the way to the dining room and there on the large table and on the kitchen counter stand more than 30 of her prized apple-head dolls waiting for us. These are the ones that she doesn't want to sell. She's kept them because she likes them too much. Some others are in the Museum of American Folk Art in New York City, but not these. They are a special population and her own small world.

———————

Now look at those! Are they old ones?

These are very old. They turn black, you see. This was a Baldwin apple and they turn black. They're old as the hills. But they make nice little tomtens, don't they?

Do you always use Baldwins?

Oh, no, I don't like them. I use Yellow Delicious because I like the shape and the skin tones.

I'm having trouble getting [miniature] chairs and things now. I have them made, but the people who make them are retiring, all these people are *retiring!* Like this rocking chair. I can't get those anymore. It's kind of cramping my style.

Well, I guess it is.

Now this is a nice chair. It's a ladderback. Can't get those anymore. So I'm not making any more dolls.

That's a shame. They're so wonderful. When you do make them, how do you start out? Does it have to be a perfect apple?

Oh, yes. No bruises. First, they're peeled and then dipped in lemon juice and some salt on them. Then you hang them up to dry. It takes about four weeks for them to dehydrate because, I think, there's two-thirds water in an apple. So all the water is dried out and nothing but the pulp is left.

What about the seeds? They're in there, too?

The core is left inside.

Then what do you do after that?

Well, I'm a sculptor anyway. I do a lot of sculpting on them and clipping, working this way and that with my fingers to shape the faces. And I use nice materials for the clothes and everything. It's all made by hand. Yep.

All parts of the clothes are made by hand?

I make all of these things, yep. There's a little lace on the bottom of some, see? The legs are made of clay.

Look at this one!

That's Mrs. Pitkin. Yep.

CARVING APPLE-HEAD DOLLS

Very nicely done. Do you paint the eyes on?

No, they're little pins, what do we call them, tack pins, are they? Matt pins about so big. Black. Yep. My daughter made that chair. A retired Army nurse.

How did you get interested in making your first one?

That's an interesting story. I was on this island off the coast of Maine, the furthermost island off the coast of Maine. Matinicus. When I was there, met a little lady who was a craftsman. She had a magazine with pictures in it and there was an apple-head doll and the body was a bottle. I saw that and I said I wonder if I could do that. So I came home and went out to the country there and bought a bushel of apples! The Baldwins. And I worked on those. Gradually, I worked out my own way of doing things.

How many different styles and characters do you have here?

Well, there's Betsy Ross here, Mrs. Pitkin, The Doctor, and Charlie Weaver, Einstein with all his hair, and Mark Twain, Mother Goose, The Scotsman over there. That's very old. See how black that is. That's an old Baldwin.

Ah, there's a hurdy-gurdy and a monkey.

Yep, that's very old. The man who makes the chair has retired so I'm up a creek without a paddle now. There's a lobster fisherman.

Now that's quite a scene.

That's an authentic net. I pulled that up out of the sand off the coast of Maine. And there's The Sailmaker and there's The Captain. Jack Tack. The Boys on the Bench. And this is Charlie Weaver. Remember him?

Yes, I do, as a matter of fact.

Now that's a nice little chair with all the spindles. They don't make those things anymore. Over here there's a pianist and a violinist.

Do the musicians have names, too?

Yes, they do. Let's see, that's Tchaikovsky. Now who's the violinist?

Heifitz?

Yes, Heifitz. Oh, he was young, I remember him when he was young. No, I forget who he is. My daughter made this spinning wheel. And this cobbler is old, very old.

Like 30 years old?

I should say so. Quite awhile.

———

Apple-head dolls are traced back to the Seneca Indians of what is now New York State. The custom, as Adalyn relates, was to pare and core the apple, place a stake that had been wrapped with feathers into the core opening, and as the apple dried, it tightened and clung to the stake. The Senecas considered them "good luck" heads and placed them in the blankets of the newborn child. This endowed the child with powers to prophesy.

Then the frontier women adopted the idea. They made the apple stakes into more elaborate figures that became dolls for their own children.

———

How long does it take you to make one doll?

Well, it takes four weeks for the head to dehydrate. In the meantime, I'm making the frame, it's all made by hand. That's

CARVING APPLE-HEAD DOLLS

wire. That's padded with cloth. They don't break, that's the nice thing.

Then I use felt for the hands and feet. Some dollmakers use apples to make the hands, but they look like claws and I didn't like those. I use this kind. I make the hats. I took a course in millinery; I'm a dressmaker so that all helps.

I make characters. I like to make characters. Like Mother Goose with the goose there, too. I use nice materials. This coat on her is part of my own suit. I use lace.

Have you sold a number of them?

Oh, yes. Over the years I've sold quite a few.

How much do they sell for?

About 35 dollars anyway, and up. A lot of work goes into them, you know. I use nice materials, very nice materials.

They don't like humidity. They soften up. I made a lot for my daughter down in Florida and they're ruined, they're just *ruined.* Oh, it's horrible.

Would the summer affect them here, too?

It would, yeah. I keep them all covered up with plastic and in the closet where it's cool and dark.

Which ones are more expensive?

Oh, the Lobster Fisherman. He'd be 45 dollars with the lobster trap and all the work that goes into. Oh, this hunter is very old. He doesn't see the pheasant right there sitting on the fence! He's looking the other way, you know. Some of these I wouldn't sell, like that one.

They're your favorites?

Yes, and I couldn't get any more. And here's Mr. Santa.

ADALYN DANIELS   157

I make characters. I like to make characters.

You said on the phone that you have some in the Museum of American Folk Art in New York. How did that come about?

She bought quite a few of them. I don't know, a girl came who works up there. I met her over at Strawbery Banke, I had some dolls over there. You know Strawbery Banke?

Yes, it's the preservation park in Portsmouth. Old colonial houses.

I was showing them over there and she fell in love with them. She bought quite a few. I had interviews and was on television at Strawbery Banke. She's been one of my best customers. She bought an awful lot of them. She comes right here, all the way from New York.

That's wonderful. She must think a lot of your work.

She may come again, I don't know. Some I won't sell. In fact, she wants this one, the Boys on the Bench, but I won't sell that. That little basket, isn't that nice? I can't get these little baskets and chairs anymore. The people are all *retired*.

They just can't keep up with you, I guess! [She laughs and takes out more dolls from a large carton.] *You must have 30 different characters here alone. Are there any other people making these?*

Not around here. A lot of people are making them, but not the way I make them. I'm an artist, a born artist. Come in here and see my stuff.

———

She leads the way down a hall. An elegant Chinese print with calligraphy hangs on the most conspicuous wall. "Isn't that nice?" she says as we pass.

Her room is crowded with redecorated furniture, busts, painted tins, prints on the walls and a very fine portrait by her daughter Scottie. Adalyn used to restore furniture. A Pennsylvania Dutch cabinet stands against one wall, a Swedish table against another, both of which are painted bright and cheerful green and yellow. She points to some of the horsehead sculptures she's done. "I like horses," she says straight out. She offers lots to look at and she's having fun showing it.

I can see that you put some extra quality into your dolls that others don't have.

Yes, I think so. I took a course in millinery, I guess I told you that. I work in clay and sculpture, and I'm a painter. So that's the story.

Have you taught others this art?

No, I haven't taught.

I hope it's not going to be a lost art. It isn't, is it?

People in different parts of the country are still doing it, but they have their own type. You see, I'm making my own old New England types.

How many do you think you've made over the years?

Oh, couple hundred maybe. Two or three hundred. I'm kind of loafing around now, not doing much.

May I take some pictures of these? And you, too?

Me? You don't want me? Do I look like one of these old dolls?

She picks out some of the dolls for the pictures, arranges the dresses just right, the jackets just perfectly. She makes her dolls with

It's about time I got them out and looked them over. See if they're all right. Check on them. Let them know I'm still thinking of them.

smiles on their faces. The world's happy when people smile, and the same should be with the apple-head dolls. No crimped-face sourpusses for her little people. That's her philosophy.

The Peddler Woman carries a tray of items for sale. Adalyn explains what's in the tray—rolling pin, Bible, buttons, a doll, ribbon, pin cushion. She arranges The Doctor with the stethoscope and Mark Twain with his frizzy hair.

ADALYN DANIELS

What is the hair?

Lamb's wool.

And you have just nice subtle coloring of the lips.

Yes, I tint those ever so slightly with paint.

How do you have so much life at 92?

I have to keep busy, you know. Keep working. Yep. I'm kind of slowing down now. I cook. I'm "chief cook and bottlewasher." Now what's this going to be in?

A book about interesting people who do interesting things in New England.

New Englanders?

Yes.

Oh, good. Good.

Do you have a very favorite doll?

No, I don't think so. Of course, I like Betsy Ross a lot.

Is there one that you made a lot more of than others?

Yes, I think so. Jack Tack and The Captain and the Lobster Fisherman. I made quite a few of those. Mark Twain is popular. I used to go to shows and fairs and show them. I still get notices of the fairs, you know. It's hard work, pack all these things and unpack them. Answer questions all day.

Just like you're doing now!

Oh, well, this is different. I had them put away in my closet there. It's about time I got them out and looked them over. See if they're all right. Check on them. Let them know I'm still thinking of them.

ELIOT COLEMAN

Small Farming

Eliot Coleman

Vershire Center, Vermont

Getting to Eliot Coleman is first driving along the tight tree-lined valley that the clear-water Ompompanoosuc River is still geologically carving. Houses with large nearby wood piles cling to the sides of the narrow valley. Mailboxes have names like Tucker, Snow, Matton, Lafevre. Roads have names like Eagle Hollow and Darling Hill. Go through Vershire, turn left on a dirt road, and climb the hill to Vershire Center, which for all practical purposes is the Mountain School, a boarding school.

Eliot Coleman is one of a kind. He's energetic, imaginative, experimental, tells a good story, uses a good image, works, works, works. He loves research, he loves knowing what he's talking about, he's generous with ideas, and most of all he loves farming.

In the 1970s he carved out a showplace small organic farm from the tangled thick Maine woods next to Helen and Scott Nearing, the inspiration for him and thousands of others interested in the good life. This farm produced extraordinary vegetables and drew customers from 20 miles away for the superb lettuce, cabbage, carrots, onions, and everything else. Old-timers and U.S. Department of Agriculture experts were coming to *him*. How does he do it? Look at those vegetables! And he's making money besides.

Then from 1978 to 1981 he directed a demonstration project for small farmers at the Coolidge Center in Topsfield, Massachusetts. Here is where he developed "the New MacDonald's Farm" system to bring more small farmers back to New England with a method that gives them a decent living.

For two years at the Mountain School in Vershire Center, Eliot has been improving a long-term tradition of providing nearly 100 percent of the food needed by the school by producing it on the school grounds. It's extraordinary.

At his "hobby" garden for his own family of Gerry and three children, he talks of the New MacDonald's Farm, growing food for institutions, and reinvigorating farming in New England. First, he points out that, "believe it or not, I can plant and chew gum at the same time."

───────────────

Did you start out with organic farming and gardening from the beginning?

At the time, the USDA was putting out literature trying to put down organic agriculture. Nitrogen was nitrogen, it didn't matter whether it came out of a bag or from a manure pile. The unsaid saying behind this was that organic is foolish, buy it out of a bag, it's just as good. The funny thing that struck me was that the USDA was saying, It's just as good either way. So to me they were saying that if you don't have the money to buy it out of a bag, it's just as good to get it from a manure pile.

Of course, using manure is the old-time method.

I suspect it all started in antiquity when primitive man would settle in an area and found out when he dropped a grain of wheat where everyone outside the hovel had taken a crap. Then after awhile they noticed the same thing with the animal manure. Of course, it's a bad idea for human beings to plant in their own.

There are two interesting books on agriculture in China— F. H. King's *Farmers of Forty Centuries* that inspired a lot of organic people. He went there in 1911. He found out that the Chinese had grown organic for 40 centuries. The second book was *Health and Agriculture in China* by James Cameron Scott. Now as far as whether manure is old-fashioned, yeah, it is, but other things are just as old-fashioned going back to the Romans. Green manures, crop rotations—and I'm convinced that you can run an organic farm with *no* animal manure. In fact, I've seen one in Europe, running just with crop rotation and green manures.

No chemicals of any kind?

I didn't say no fertilizers, I said no manures. The way people are doing it now is that you're sowing in clover right in your standing crop. So even in Vershire, Vermont, when after I harvest corn I barely have time to get rye in, I put the clover in in the third week of June and that's been growing as an understory of the corn. I take the corn off and I've got a clover field. So next spring whatever follows the corn in rotation, like potatoes, I've got clover to plow under without ever having to worry about the fact that it's too cold.

Very clever.

Well, good organic farming today is old technology with new twists. I talked with a New Jersey farmer and he said, Oh, yes, we did that with hairy clover back in Oughty Seven!

It's good to have young people from the suburbs see a farm in operation, like what you have here at the Mountain School.

People are often totally ignorant of where their food comes from. In fact, I think some of the most ignorant people are in the universities, actually. I've seen studies done by ag[riculture] people in which they are convinced that Vermont at best could produce between 6 to 20 percent of its food. The Mountain School has been sitting here for 20 years growing about 95 percent of its food. Right here we're at 1,650 feet elevation. The garden is up on top of the hill at 1,700 feet. It's cold here.

But you actually produce enough food?

They've always fed their students. They have beef, a flock of Romney sheep, 24 lambs running out, a couple of sows and boar, and every spring they would buy between four and six calves.

And the garden provides the vegetables.

Yes. I reorganized it this past year. It wasn't quite as efficient as it should have been. There was very often too much of one

. . . good organic farming today is old technology with new twists.

thing and not enough of the other. One year there was nothing but snow peas. We taught a course last year on institutional food production and also a whole garden plan on how to set up a rotation to make sure you got the proper quantities of each of the vegetables. The beauty of the system is that we don't run it with a tractor, although the school has a tractor. I'm trying to encourage other schools to use this method. It's just a walking tractor, a large-scale rototiller, anything from a 6-horsepower to a 14-horsepower Italian one that I used on a project in Massachusetts.

Is that sufficiently big enough to handle a small farm?

168   SMALL FARMING

That will handle five acres of vegetables, the 14-horsepower. The 6-horse, like the Troybilt, you could push that to two acres.

How much does the total cost turn about to be?

The total cost for five acres to feed 200 people is 5,000 dollars. That's buying all your equipment brand new. Amortizing that equipment over five years, plus interest, plus what you pay every year for seed and rock fertilizer or whatever you're buying, it comes out to 10 dollars per person per year. Total cost.

That's fantastic. Is that accurate?

Absolutely. The reason it's so neat is that people think in terms of incredible amounts of equipment, which you don't need. It's equipment we found while I was at the Coolidge Center. It's stuff to help the small farmer get into business. We couldn't tell him that he needed 20,000 dollars for equipment.

We also didn't want to tell him to buy used equipment, because we wanted to set up a system that wasn't going to be stopped when the used equipment ran out. So we found a lot of walking tractors. We found a one-row, hand-pushed seeder in Sweden that probably was one of the keys to the operation. It puts in arrow-straight rows of any spacing you want, any type seed you want. So if you think of carrots, which are a real pain in the butt, because, first you have to thin them and then weed in the row because you can't get close enough to them. This seeder puts in a seed every inch or whatever you set it.

One carrot seed?

One carrot seed, yes. Then another piece of equipment can get you within a half-inch of plants for weeding. So I'm leaving myself a half-inch of hand weeding. It's the most incredibly efficient little system you've ever seen in your life.

Eliot's "hobby" garden has had lettuce and spinach growing under glass since early spring. They are utterly fantastic leaf greens— healthy, vivid, *perfect*. Currently, he's experimenting with someone's idea of plastic pyramids holding water around seedlings to help them grow by trapped heat from the sun. They work if the sun is out.

Gerry arrives in the car with four turkey chicks. We all huddle around while Gerry and Eliot put the turkeys in a warm area inside the school building; 49 three-week-old chickens chirp in the adjoining platform.

The Mountain School was originally a farm in the mid-1800s. In the 1950s it was a dairy farm, then since 1963 a high-standard boarding school. Its new life stems from being sold to the Milton Academy in Massachusetts. With a consortium of nine other schools, it will run a junior year in the country for students.

Can you extend that 95 percent growing your own institutional food right here to all of Vermont or New England? Is growing that much food feasible for here?

I'm convinced it is. What we don't have is the incentive to do it. We worked all these things out in Topsfield and we worked it out very simply. When I took that job, I was told that the aim of the project was to get more farmers back in business. I said that's great, that's simple. Let's double food prices. They'll stumble over themselves to get back in business. Obviously, we can't do that, if you understand economics. So we've got two things we can do. We can either get them a maximum price for their product, which means that they're going to sell retail rather than wholesale. Or we're going to lower the production costs. A hell of a lot more people can keep a lawn mower running, which is basically like the walking tractor, than a tractor diesel.

Did you see any progress of getting farmers back in operation in New England while you were there at Topsfield?

Oh, yeah. The concept has to be carried one step further. We were working on the practical aspect. Then there is the social aspect. It's a really interesting thing. Say you're giving a cocktail party. You tell your guests proudly, See the nice tomato slices at the end of the table: I grew them. You're cool! Now you say proudly, I grow all the food that we eat here for the year. All of a sudden the conversation drops away, everybody looks at the wall, and they go home five minutes later.

Your wife's at the cocktail party. She proudly announces, I made this dress myself, and everybody claps. Then she announces, I make all the clothes for our family, and the same reaction happens as before. Farmers are the low, low end of the totem pole.

I did some consulting work and I came across a program at a convention of the American Guidance Counseling Association. There were approximately 700 workshops presented there on guiding kids into professions. One was on agriculture and that one was titled "Guidance Counselors Can Guide Minority Students *Even* Into Agriculture."

It's such an ill-recognized value. You know that the strength of any country is based on its food.

Obviously. Think about another thing. What does the USDA announce every year more proudly than they announce anything else? They announced proudly that last year 4.5 percent of the working population were farmers. Now we have it down to 4.2 percent and the way things are going it'll be down to 3.9 percent. They're talking about a problem with leprosy.

What do you tell people who are interested in going back into small farming? What do you suggest they do?

The State of Maine when I was there got interested in helping small farmers and one guy asked me what I thought about the courses that should be held. He was thinking of a soils course and a course on how to make compost. I said what you ought to hold is a course in small business management. Every backwoodsman in Maine knows how to grow corn and vegetables. He's been doing it all his life. What he doesn't know is how to turn it into a business.

ELIOT COLEMAN

Good point.

You can take my farm in Maine as an example. We grew 40 varieties of vegetables. We figured out very quickly that when people are going to drive six miles out to our farm they want not just lettuce but somewhere they can get everything, everything all the time. That meant growing eight varieties of cabbage ripening over a long period of time, so we had it whenever it came in to the end of the season.

I once calculated that we had 130 different models of our 40 different varieties of vegetables. Now there are very few small businessmen that are running anything that complicated. It turns out that it takes a hell of a lot more ability to run a successful small farm than to run 85 percent of the small businesses. Now nobody is going to admit that because the farmer was always the dumb kid who couldn't get into law school or become a priest or become a doctor.

Now that's why I got thinking about Ray Kroc. Ray Kroc made it possible for a lot of dummies who could never have succeeded running a hamburger stand to make themselves a bloody fortune.

The one who developed MacDonalds.

Ray Kroc more than anything else was a very good synthesizer and teacher.

And that's what you're talking about—systems.

Definitely. He was selling milkshake blenders and they had one model that made eight at a time. He sold them all over the country, he was a salesman for them. This outfit in California bought 18 of them. He said, Man, I've got to go out and *see* that place. It was the MacDonalds brothers and they had the most fantastic fast food stand he had ever seen in his life. So he bought them out and sat down to copy all their secrets—*everything*, because they had done a lot of thinking about this.

Anyway, he came up with a way for any idiot with a street corner location and the capital to buy a franchise to succeed

172

because all that sort of thinking had been done. And what we were about to turn out in Topsfield, and would have turned out if the people who had the money weren't such total idiots, was what was going to be what we called our New MacDonald's farm.

Which would have been what?

How to be a small farmer; you buy these *three* pieces of equipment; you plant *only* these ten crops because they're the most remunerative; here's the rotation you plant them in (and the dates are relative one to the other because of the differences in New Hampshire and New Jersey); these are the sales containers you need; we calculate that for that acreage of broccoli you're going to have to hire two pickers, and so forth. Everything was going to be right there, exactly the same way.

I was convinced that that information in a book in your hands would let you succeed with a small farm the same way you would running a hamburger stand.

Eliot is working on a book about his ideas for the New Mac-Donald's farm as they apply to institutional and small-farm production. They're important ideas and they could make a significant improvement in small farms not only in New England but across the country.

Such a system of institutional food growing can be used not only for schools but for prisons, monasteries, community groups, even small towns—anybody who wants to get together and develop a food-growing system at minimal cost.

In his upstairs office, we talk of the many tools he brings back from trips to Europe and England. Ingenious weeders. Hoes with angles that keep your back straight. Spades with two shoulder-high handles so you won't break your back. Potting-soil cube makers. Clever seeders.

What is the most important tool?

This seeder is what made everything possible, getting seeds in efficiently. One person with three tools, the seeder, the rototiller, and cultivator, could handle five acres, only doing the growing. Planting, growing, and marketing are the three parts. For planting, we give you this New MacDonald farm book. For growing—there are 38 million home food gardens in this country so this is neither an unknown nor esoteric activity. And marketing—that is 50 percent of the successful small farmer. It made us in Maine, not just because we knew how to grow it but we knew how to market it.

How long did it take for you to establish a market in Maine?

Our income there, with no advertising other than a sign at our entrance, went from 400 dollars to 1,200 dollars, 2,600 dollars, 4,000 dollars to 5,500 dollars. That was the progression in five years.

Did you increase the acreage? From what to what?

From zero to five acres of vegetables. Actually, a lot of that was fodder beets grown for stock feed and not for sale. The soil was so poor that we had to make it before we could make money on it. But because of that, I learned a hell of a lot more of what soil fertility is composed of. I had to make it or nothing would grow. I couldn't have picked a better spot to get my education.

Overall, the country has produced a lot of wheat and corn with chemical fertilizers.

A lot of things go on. I was told by an Englishman that governments push the sale of chemical fertilizer because nitrogen fertilizer and gunpowder are made in the same factory and process. After the war it was very uncomfortable for governments to have a lot of gunpowder factories. Well, not being a conspiracy theorist, I said, Well, yes, that's very interesting, I'm sure you invented that, I don't think things like that are true.

Then I happened to be looking through the 1938 yearbook of the Department of Agriculture and I came upon a chapter and, lo and behold, this is what was said [reads from book]: "The influence of the war on the production of new fertilizer . . . the system demand for propellant powders . . . huge chemical plants were erected to meet the requirements. . . . When the world war was terminated the huge chemical plants geared to capacity production of wartime necessities faced a difficult situation." Right there in the book! So my English friend was right.

What we don't know!

So where did DDT and the start of all those come from? From World War II also. Your huge chemical concerns find they have a hell of a market there. They captured the minds of the people at the universities. If I've learned anything, it's that my understanding of agriculture does not capture the average mind because it loves to be captured by simple solutions. If you have a headache, what do you do? You take an aspirin. You don't think, hmm, I wonder if my hat is too tight. You don't bother to go through the cause-and-effect thing. You get rid of the symptom right off.

When DDT came in, it was unbelievable. A load of nitrogen in your soil in the first year or two doubled your crops. But then you break down a lot of your organic matter and structure and it takes more and more nitrogen to work, but nobody was paying attention at that point.

Now to your point. Yes, we have an incredibly productive agriculture in the U.S., but it is only dependably productive in the staples—wheat, soybeans, corn, and cotton, I suppose. The indications are that by the year 2000 California will need all its agriculture to feed itself. They won't be exporting anything. That was part of the New England states saying, Hey, maybe we ought to stimulate the local agriculture.

Can a small farmer sell at the supermarket price and still make a decent living?

Not as a small farmer in the wholesale market because then you're supporting that fat profit for the guy in the middle. If you can retail your stuff, you can make out like a bandit. We used to kid in Maine that we could make 100,000 dollars an acre just in lettuce. It was pseudotrue. An acre is 43,560 square feet. Call it

40,000. We put a head of lettuce in a square foot. That's 40,000 lettuces. One planting of lettuce. Sell it for 50 cents a head and you've got 20,000 dollars. But we do ours on a transplant system. Lettuce is 60 days from seed to harvest. Our lettuces spend the first 30 days in the flat before we transfer them out. So our lettuce needs only 30 days in the ground. We have a five-month growing season in Maine. We could repeat that 40,000 lettuces five times. And there was our 100,000 dollars a year off one acre!

Perfect.

There is a lot of money in an efficiently run vegetable operation. There's also a lot of bullshit like I just told you, articles on living off an acre. What was Eisenhower's great quote? Farming looks nice and easy when the plow is a pencil and you're 1,000 miles from the cornfield.

What you need are innovative minds in agriculture. In Japan some organic farmers have subscription farms. A farmer may have 20 people to supply them food and provide him a year-round income. The people would become attached to their farm and come out to weed on the weekend. Now that's a hell of a relationship. And when you have only one farmer in 20 people, you really have only 5 percent of your population as farmers! So there aren't too many lepers around.

Farming becomes acceptable.

When I travel I don't go to art museums, I go to hardware stores. There is so much technology around the world that's being ignored. We have a lack of imagination on scale. We thought that bigger was better because it's so easier to see bigger.

In Europe, and I really learned a lot over there, the small farmer is a respected member of society. They never had a California, so the small farm never died out.

———

Farming in Vermont has its problems with weather. On April 26 Eliot snapped a picture of the kids skiing on the farm. That morning, 200 yards away, he'd been plowing the garden.

What was Eisenhower's great quote? Farming looks nice and easy when the plow is a pencil and you're 1,000 miles from the cornfield.

After working at Coolidge Center in Topsfield, he was told that what he was doing would be impossible in a moist climate with 18 generations of bugs. "So when I got a chance to work on a moist warm farm with 18 generations of bugs," he says, "I jumped on it."

He and Gerry headed for northeast Texas. After two and a half months they looked at each other across a crowded room and assessed the Texas scene as not for them. They headed back to New England.

We talk awhile on the 1.5-acre hilltop garden plot. The White Mountains in New Hampshire on the east side of the Connecticut River shimmer through the long horizon. The nearby land is tree-wild and isolated, except for the cleared fields of the Mountain School below where very woolly sheep have the big slanting fields to them-selves.

Is the organic movement better organized now, do you think?

I don't know. When I was starting in Maine, organic groups were young and vigorous and idealistic. Now they are older, more mature, and less energetic. Like any institutionalized idea. I'm not sure they're as effective. It's gotten a following but it's a following like a fundamentalist church would get and it really doesn't grow except when its members have kids.

It's like preaching to those who are already committed.

Yes, like that. I don't know whether I like the word *movement* either. I like clear thinking and so far agriculture hasn't been thinking clearly. It's been doing unnecessary things because it's been easy.

I have a standing bet when I lecture at universities that, OK, give me your most recalcitrant professor with one hour and a six-pack of beer. I guarantee you I'll straighten out his head, and I never lost that bet. It isn't that I turn him into a believer; I merely explain to him that the ideas behind what good organic farmers are doing are just as sound agronomy as the ideas of what a big chemical farmer is doing.

With that we walk the winding hillside road down to dinner. "Good farms are really good gardens," he says on the way. Gerry is busy fixing us an irresistibly delicious dinner and when the five of us sit down it's oh's and ah's at seeing the fresh colorful whole-someness of it all displayed in bowls and plates and dishes. And the spinach and lettuce! He *is* the Picasso of farming.

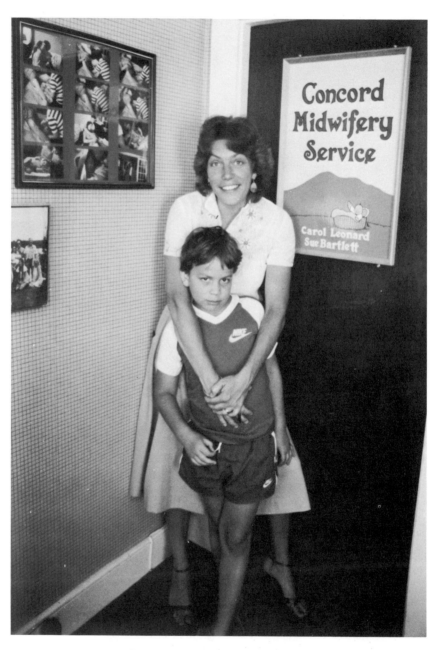

CAROL LEONARD AND SON MILAN

Midwifery

Carol Leonard

Concord, New Hampshire

Being born at home has been going on since the beginning of the species, and women assisting women in childbirth is equally an ancient tradition and practice. Only in modern times has the hospital birth usurped this most natural process. Since nearly everyone today is born in a hospital, merely the thought of a home birth seems extraordinary.

Comes now a growing return to home births with midwives as assistants, and one of the most significant areas for this revival of more natural childbirth is New Hampshire. Midwifery is outlawed in Massachusetts, across the southern border, but in New Hampshire Carol Leonard has been an active beacon for those women and men who see birth as natural, not an aberration, and who therefore think that the setting should be as natural as possible, too. Carol was the first midwife in the state in recent times, has delivered more than 800 babies, conducts her own midwifery program with her partner Susan Bartlett, and is on the executive board of the Midwife Alliance of North America.

A sign in her office reads: "Concord Midwifery Service—For a Special Delivery." Outside on the porch she talks of midwifery in America today and how she started her practice.

Most of our grandmothers delivered our mothers and fathers in the home, but I see that now about 95 percent of births are in hospitals. Why are you so involved in home births? How did it all begin for you?

I had my son Milan in a hospital and my body was fine, but the whole hospital routine, which I had been prepared for, made me realize that American women were really being manipulated and coopted into thinking that that was childbirth. There was nothing natural about it, except that I didn't have any drugs. It was horrible.

I had a very easy short labor, but I was pushing flat on my back and strapped down. I remember putting my hand between my legs because it was burning when his head was beginning to crown and the doctor slapped my hand back and said it was a sterile field. He tied my hands down and I thought, my crotch wasn't sterile when I came in here, I don't know why it's sterile now.

When you don't have any drugs and you're good, they allowed you to look in this mirror. I remember in childbirth classes they said, You never question the doctor. And I never questioned that. It all came together at the same point and I said, Give me my baby. The nurse said, Oh, no, you have flat nipples or something. I was really angry. I said, Give me my baby! I was really growling and I think they thought I was postpartum psychotic.

So that started you thinking about the whole American childbirth scene?

That was the beginning. I had no plans of being a midwife. After Milan was born I was reading every obstetrical book I could get my hands on. I went to the Feminist Health Center here and convinced them they should hire me, and they did. They trained me as a sort of paramedic doing a lot of family planning. Then I approached this wonderful old country doctor, Francis Brown. He was the only doctor in the state that was doing home births. He was great. I asked him if I could tag along as a shadow and I was really surprised when he said absolutely. He was getting older and he wanted someone to be his assistant. Actually, it was from him that I learned the art. It was an art that was really being lost because in medical school they don't teach you all those commonsense maneuvers.

I did 50 babies with him. We worked together a long time. He really enjoyed woman-to-woman interaction. So actually, when I started working with him, he didn't catch another baby, I don't think; he was just a teacher, a mentor. Then in the midst of that, people started calling me and I started putting together this little birth bag, this kit. I was with Dr. Brown with a breach birth in Hillsboro and I got paged to go to my first birth way up in Ossipee. It was the lady's first birth and out in the woods and I remembered being so terrified driving up there. I had diarrhea, I had to stop three times!

How did it turn out?

Great. It seemed that nothing ever happened complicationwise until I had learned already how to deal with it.

Have you delivered in log cabins and the like?

Oh, yeah. I remember at the beginning delivering in a teepee where the woman tore and there were just the two of us and I had to repair the laceration holding a flashlight between my teeth. That was back in the crazy days. We don't practice alone anymore.

Have you lost any?

I haven't lost one yet.

At the time Carol was first practicing, midwifery was not recognized or even thought of, let alone legal. In some emergencies, she probably could have been accused of practicing medicine without a license, she says, but the incidents were rare.

As the first midwife in the state, she began training others. The second midwife came to work with her in the summer and fall and that was the year they helped with 160 babies. Clearly, they were filling a need. Women and their men wanted to give birth to their children in their own home and surrounded by a familiar scene of caring and loving relatives and friends.

The second midwife is on the state advisory board for public health. Now 24 midwives are practicing in New Hampshire through the revival that Carol spawned, and more are being trained.

Do you perform episiotomies?

No. The only reason we do them here is for some reason the baby's heart is sounding low and we want to get the baby out

CAROL LEONARD

faster than having him crown naturally, and that's really rare. Probably less than a dozen a year. We wouldn't routinely do them because they look like they're going to tear. Our philosophy is that usually when someone is going to have a tear, it involves much less muscle damage than an episiotomy. It's easier to repair. This whole thing that episiotomies are much easier to repair I don't find to be true.

I think that where a lot of these episiotomies came from is that watching the crowning makes men cross their legs. It hurts them to watch, and I think they want to do something to help. For the women, on the other hand, it's so powerful at that point. It's something you're caught up into. You're numb and at the same time sort of orgasmic and it makes it anticlimactic to have an episiotomy at that moment.

What are the risks of a home birth that women have to be especially aware of as opposed to a hospital birth?

I think the main thing with home deliveries is complete comprehensive care. That's what we do here. We screen out I'd say 97 percent of the complications that can occur. We don't do someone at home who has a medical history that can complicate a birth. We won't do twins, we won't do malpresentations. We have really good medical backup. When a woman has to go to the hospital, we do go with them.

We do a lot of first babies. There's always a lot of crying about an untested pelvis, but I still think that if a woman squats versus being flat on her back in the hospital, it's better. We don't carry forceps, we don't need them. You just use the basic physiological process and respect that. We have them squat to open their pelvis and use gravity. Sir Isaac Newton figured it out.

His mother, too. Do you think you've had any influence, through your 800 births, on doctors and hospitals around here?

Oh, yes, absolutely. There's been a whole change. Specifically, the Concord Hospital. Back at the beginning, I went to the hospital with 33 consumer demands that needed to be changed in order to really respect the woman and the family in a birthing environment. I remember at that point the physician saying, no way, no way, no way, and checking off all of them saying, no way.

What are some of them that come to mind?

Not delivering routinely in the delivery room, delivering in the labor bed. No way. Having siblings here. No way. No routine episiotomy. No way. On and on and on. Well, now Concord Hospital has done absolutely every single one of those requests, and I do think because of that they're one of the most progressive hospitals in the United States.

Have you had any repeats?

We've had some women who have had four babies with us. As a matter of fact, I don't think we've ever had a woman who's opted for a home birth ever go to a hospital. A lot of people will come here even though they have complete insurance coverage. They'll pay out of their pocket.

Now why exactly do they opt for home birth?

I guess it's a philosophy. It's a respect. We do have medical skills available to us, but we do have a love for the women. We've had babies ourselves. It's a real respect: number one, that the woman's body can do it, and for leaving their family and environment intact.

Midwifery is the oldest profession, you know. I don't know how to explain it. It's just gotten so technological and so far away from the natural process. It is the most important thing that a woman will ever do and the most powerful thing. It is empowering . . . to allow the woman to control her own experience and her environment and having her man there and her family there, dictating how she wants it to be. Our role is to be invisible, unless they need some directions, and just ascertain that everything is not becoming complicated.

Are you the "doctor"?

No. It's more of a love, more a sister or mother, I guess. A trust. I guess it's that they hired us because they respect our

. . . it's a philosophy . . . a respect. We do have medical skills available to us, but we do have a love for the women. We've had babies ourselves. It's a real respect . . . that the woman's body can do it . . .

judgment and our expertise. If we say that we think this is becoming too abnormal and that we recommend that you go to a hospital, they'll go because that's why they hired us. It's intuition that we use a lot. It's a feeling that we use a lot, that things are going well or not well. Susie and I have developed that to a fine tune. We respect it and we respect it in each other. If one or the other gets a feeling that things are getting bad, we never argue that, never. We've always been right on, even though there's never been any medical indication. Sometimes it scares some of the doctors.

All this may be something a little alien to some doctors.

Yeah, it is.

Are you—midwifery in general—a threat to the profession in a way?

I think it's growing and some egos are involved and maybe some financial things. It seems to be better here in New Hampshire, but when I travel all over the United States and I talk to other midwives, it's terrible. In a lot of other places, a lot of midwives are being persecuted. It's still a witchhunt. It's a modern-day twentieth-century witchhunt. What's happening in New Hampshire is phenomenal. We've set up the New Hampshire Midwives Association and banded together and got strong, even though it's small. Then we push to pass legislation and there was legislation passed that we fought for desperately in 1981. It sets up an advisory committee to the director of public health to set up rules and regulations for the legal practice of the profession of lay midwifery. We're the seventh state in the nation to do that.

In New Hampshire? That's astounding.

Yeah, you bet. Part of that is that we gave our statistics and all the physicians came to the legislative hearing shouting and yelling about all our damaged babies at home, our vegetable babies. Half of the legislators are old and *they* were all born at home! They were really offended!

Also New Hampshire has the largest percentages of women in its legislature in the country. Did that help?

It could. Also, the people of New Hampshire are fiercely independent. In other states the AMA and the medical lobby are very powerful and have a lot of money. In this state the people aren't so impressed with the medical model. Some of the old New Hampshire Yankee came through.

Some doctors now use a birthing chair that midwives had used for centuries. In those days men were not allowed at a birth. Then King Louis XIV of France, voyeur that he was and forbidden from the birthing chamber, required that his mistresses lie flat on their backs so he could peek around a curtain and see. So—the story goes— evolved the practice of mothers delivering their children in a supine position. It's easier for the practitioner and the attendant but not for the woman.

"It's funny," Carol says, "how many of these medical practices that are called medical haven't any physiological consideration at all. They're just habit."

In her practice, Carol sees very little postpartum depression in home births where the rooms are familiar and the people so involved. When she foresees the need for a Caesarian section, she transfers the mother to a hospital, but this happens only about 6 percent of the time and usually for a first child. Overall, she says, her complication rate is 3 to 5 percent, and most of the time the problems are handled at home.

Is it standard to have brothers and sisters at the births?

For us, it's standard and we love it. We really encourage that. We think that it creates an important bond between the siblings and the new one. We don't make the child be there. There has to be one other person there to specifically feel out the child's reaction. The kids have their face in there so close that you have to struggle for elbow room yourself. And they help. They're so wonderful.

It must create a real understanding of birth.

The young ones don't have any innate hang-up about births. I think that comes much, much later. Kids nine or ten, you may have to do more explaining, but young kids don't have any fear. They don't have a hang-up about the vagina or blood, maybe blood once in awhile. What we say to the little ones is that it's good blood, it's been feeding the baby and what was keeping the baby alive, it's not a hurt blood.

The question of sterility must crop up a lot.

Oh, if you consider the fact that even in the dirtiest home, the woman and the children have autoimmunity in their own home. In the hospitals sterility is really a joke, especially with some of these superinfections they get. You can't really go in and power blast all those bugs in the delivery room. It'll *look* sterile. And some of our houses do *not* look sterile.

What about disadvantages? What are some disadvantages of home births?

One of them, I think, is that if a woman needs a lot of rest and she's got five other kids, that's a real issue. She can stay in a hospital and rest and get pampered and waited on. At home we really require, if she has other kids, that someone be there as a live-in for a week and help.

Over and above the man.

Yeah, because some of these supermoms jump up and do the laundry and cooking and chase after the other kids. And after a home birth you feel good and it makes you feel like you can do it.

Have you seen any changes in the background of women choosing a home birth?

In the beginning most people opting for home births were, what they called the lunatic fringe, the organic back-to-the-land people, self-sufficient, goat-milk drinkers. But now a lot are young professionals, lawyers, insurance people. I don't know whether it's because the goat-milk crowd grew up. I was a wild hippie type back then, too. You just kind of mature. I think that's what happened to the whole movement; it's matured.

CAROL LEONARD

189

What about the future? What would you like to see happen?

I think we're in the midst of a real subtle revolution, a medical upheaval. It's indicative of what's going to happen as far as self-care as opposed to this patriarch approach to medicine. We are at the beginning. There is a witchhunt and we're being persecuted. I think there's going to be a big battle.

A survey profiles the typical woman having a home birth with Carol and her partner Susan as a 27-year-old with two and a half years of college. About 80 percent of these take childbirth-preparation classes; they end up with a child born at an average eight and a half pounds, more than the national average.

A home birth through Carol as midwife now costs $600. This would be the doctor's fee; the hospital fee is eliminated so that the total cost for a home birth turns out to be about one-half to one-third the average hospital cost.

Carol says that as for allowing midwifery to develop, New Hampshire "has been incredible." She and others have been working on rules and regulations under Dr. William Wallace, director of the public health for the state. She calls him "fantastic." For one thing, he's worked with midwives all over the world and understands what the reality is all about.

Do you think it's possible for that 95 percent of births in hospitals to drop to 50 percent?

Oh, yes, more than that. I think there will always be some who feel safer in a hospital. We're just trying to give some options to the standard delivery. Obstetricians are necessary when there's a higher case and we're not saying they're not. Some of us are objecting to their attitudes, and their attitudes can be pretty disgusting.

Do you see any difference between a woman OB and a man?

No. I think medical school kind of drains out your sex. A lot of women have had to deny their sex in order to survive medical school. Some of the women OBs are just as guilty of being interventionist of the process, worse sometimes actually.

Are you saying that the profession of obstetrics is a dying one?

No, I think they're necessary, maybe not the numbers, and some with the worst attitudes will probably be weeded out. They just won't be selected as the women become more educated about their bodies and the whole process. Some of them just don't respect women. It's really interesting why they select the profession when they don't have any respect for women. You have to wonder what the motivation was to get involved in the first place. I think that it's natural for women to opt for women to help them in childbirth, and I think that this drugged-up era of technological birth is ending and that women are getting back to their roots and what they really need.

CLIFF BORDEAUX AND ROBERT BORDEAUX

Cider Making

Robert Bordeaux

Cliff Bordeaux

Somers, Connecticut

The nectar of New England is a good cold aromatic sweet apple cider brimming with flavor and the crisp taste of late summer and autumn. You can't beat it, especially fresh from the press and made with care and expertise. But first you have to find a small operation by the side of the road, like what father Robert Bordeaux and son Cliff Bordeaux do.

It all started with grandfather Wilfred when he bought the mill and set it up during World War II. It was just a pile of pieces until they managed to put it together—and it worked. Originally, the mill was connected to a waterwheel at the previous location. Now it's run by a hydraulic pump.

First, apples from their own orchard are dumped on a conveyor belt outside the cider mill shed. The apples are conveyed through the second floor window and dumped into the grinder. The grinder pulps them and drops the mash into a 2-bushel holding box downstairs. Here's where the mill is run by a series of wide belts turning large iron wheels. The trap door is opened and the ground apples fall into a cloth in a frame on a rack. The frames hold 2 bushels to a cloth and build up to eight cloths, which are called a cheese. The cloth is folded over each apple-pulp supply and when all is ready the rack is slid under the press and pressure is applied slowly. The press then squeezes the juice from the apples. The juice falls into a large holding tank underneath. Finally, the juice is poured into jugs, capped, a label applied, and the jugs are taken a hundred yards away to the stand by the side of the road.

The cider mill is part of a well-kept farm of rolling fields and apple orchards. Inside the red shed, the sweet drifts of apple are constant and tempting as we talk while the mill is operating. Unless otherwise indicated, son Cliff is the one explaining how they make sweet cider.

The cloth filters the pulp from the juice, right?

The cloth is a very coarse-weave nylon. From the 1800s on the first ones they used were a burlap like a potato sack. The burlap under pressure tends to pop a lot. The nylon gives a little and is a little better. Because of the coarseness, you'll get a fine pomace that'll come through and usually collect at the bottom of the jug. That doesn't happen with nylon as much. Also, they have new grinders now that almost sauce the apples. So what they're really doing is not pressing chopped apples. They're pressing applesauce, and that tends to make a lot of pomace in the cider. The public doesn't like it that much. Sometimes a modern improvement like that doesn't work out. It's too good.

So although you're using nylon, basically, it's the old way of making cider.

Yes, it's still the old way of doing it. There's even a finer, thinner nylon. So after the cloths and rack are full—we call it a cheese at this point, a cheese of eight cloths—we wheel the cart under here to squeeze. We usually put on two squeezes. The second one we run up to maximum pressure.

How much is that?

We try to get up between 1,500 and 2,000 pounds, depending on the age of the apples and the type of apples even. You might stop at even 1,500. It's whenever the wheel stops turning, that's how we can tell. Then we slip the belt back to the grinding wheel.

Now why would the type of apples make a difference? Because they're drier or coarser?

Yes, some apples grind up a little coarser. Some tend to grind up a little softer so they tend to shift a little bit. Sometimes they tend to swim around a little once you get some pressure going.

Do you use mostly McIntosh? It's the popular apple around here.

No, we use a big variety of apples. We try to make the biggest variety we can. It makes the best cider, it gives the best flavor that way.

Which ones do you use, then?

We actually have a lot of antique apples, what we call antique, the older varieties.

Robert: The orchard was started by Grandfather. A few years ago, you know, farmers raised a few apples, raised a few cows, had a few pigs. They had a variety of everything.

When you say antique apples, do you mean Northern Spy, for example? Would you consider that antique?

That's an older apple. We have Rhode Island Greening, which is the older one, not the newer hybrids that are bred for size more than anything else. We have a few Sheep Nose. That's the original apple that the Red Delicious came from. It has a flat side on it whereas a Delicious has four flat sides basically in shape and a pointed end. This is round on one side so if you look at it in profile it looks like a sheep's nose.

Do you use a certain formula or recipe or do you just dump in whatever apples you have available at the time?

You have an idea of what all the apples taste like so you try to make a good blend of those. We have a lot of old varieties and we try to mix those in.

ROBERT AND CLIFF BORDEAUX   195

Robert: This batch has quite a few Macs, Delicious, Greenings, Nothern Spies, quince.

Cliff grafts the trees and is trying to come up with more old varieties. He's developing Red Astrakin of Russian origin and brought here in 1790. Other old ones on the farm are Spitzenburg (Thomas Jefferson's favorite), Maiden Blush, Wolf River, and Westfield Seek-No-Furthers.

It's a 150-acre farm, split into 75 acres of pasture land and orchards and the rest as woodlot. Cliff planted a new orchard about seven years ago and those antique varieties are now coming in.

Public taste in apples changes, and sometimes not always for the better. Too often varieties are developed to facilitate production, handling, and public-relations images. The Red Delicious is one example. It looks like an apple but its taste compared to some of the older apples ends up with a score of one on a scale of ten. Cliff and Robert are aiming for the taste.

Have you found that there is a certain combination that is better than others for your cider?

Yeah, we'll not tell you what it is!

Not even a hint?

Trade secret! Actually, I think what makes our cider unique is that we have the older apples and we do use them in the cider. It's a flavor you won't find in a lot of the commercial orchards because most of them make it basically from Macs and Delicious.

Robert: If you go to one of the commercial cider mills and you look at the apples they're using, you'll see something else we don't do. When I dump them, I make certain that no rotten apples go through. When you go to a commercial cider mill, they're shoveling them in. We don't believe in doing that. You put rotten apples in and rotten apples taste bad.

Cliff: This is a family operation and it's your name that's on it. So we don't have complaints. And we do have a lot of people who tell us that after comparing ciders it does stand on its own.

Robert: We have people come up from Rhode Island. Now there must be 30 million cider mills in Rhode Island. They come over here and buy cider. I mean, it kind of makes you proud.

It must. How many apples does it take for a batch?

We use 16 bushels per batch. Out of that you'll get anywhere from 35 to 50 gallons, depending the time of year, type of apples you're using. Right now we've been averaging $2^1/_2$ to 3 gallons a bushel. When you get 3 gallons a bushel, that's a pretty good year. Again, it depends on how much pressure you can squeeze them before they just won't squeeze anymore.

You press the apples very slowly.

Yes. The object is not to press too fast so your whole cheese won't be moving around too much. It doesn't force out too much of the smaller pulp through the cloth that way, although by the time you get it up to 2,000 pounds you're pushing it. It presses the apples in the cheese from about 4 inches thick to about an inch.

The holding tanks can handle about how much?

Two of them, 50 gallons a side. There's a second tank for the other side upstairs because this mill has the capacity to make about 200 gallons at a time. Really, you need a second set of people when it comes time for that—for bottling on this side and cleaning off the other. But for two people we're working about as hard as we care to.

The tank is made of cypress. The wood part of the press is all oak, including the blocking and the rack, which are oak strips. The rest is cast iron made by the A. B. Farquhar Co. This is the 1,159th one they built. It's an 1859 press.

Some of the outfits go up to a 4-bushel capacity, and some of them can press a little higher cheese.

How long does it usually take to press it out? The whole process?

It takes about 20 minutes to give it both squeezes. The whole operation takes about an hour and 15 minutes or so by the time you start grinding to when you start the next batch. We start at eight in the morning or so. Sometimes we start an hour earlier to oil up the moving parts in the mill and get everything ready so once you get started you can just keep going. On our busy weekends we did it from about eight to six at night, Saturday and Sunday.

Do you sell that much?

We sell all we can handle down here at the stand. My wife and my sister are down at the little fruit stand at the side of the house.

You don't sell it to other dealers or distributors?

No.

How much do you actually make in a day?

That again depends on the time of year. We don't really advertise. All our sales are by word of mouth and, I guess, that's poor marketing technique, but we really didn't have a need for it. We've sold everything we make. We've sold about 200 gallons on a weekend, plus about 80 or 90 bushels of apples. We go from Labor Day to Thanksgiving for cider and apples both now. We'd kind of like to extend it to Christmas. With some of the earlier antique trees we can be pressing in August. For the early varieties, that's kind of the reason they went out of favor. People aren't picking apples in August and that's when the early ones ripen up about that time. The next batch ripens up about October or so, the wintering apples like the Baldwins. They'd keep in the cellar without refrigeration, and they do keep marvelously well. That used to be our storage in the basement of the house. We'd fill it with apples and they'd keep right up into February.

You must have been making cider a long time.

I remember vague memories of when the mill was first set up. My father and grandfather would be carrying the apples upstairs in burlap sacks to put them into the grinder. I'm 28 and I say I've been doing it for 20 years, helping them along. I started following Grandpa around when I spent my summers here as a little kid. He sort of put me to work right away in the spring. I'd be picking up prunings from the trees. Then he started teaching me how to prune the trees. About seven years ago we decided that if we're going to be serious about the farm we're going to start putting in some new orchards, and we did. Grandfather showed me how to graft. About half the trees out there are all grafted, ones that he had done.

———————

His grandfather's father bought the farm in the late 1890s. His grandfather came to the farm when he was two and spent his entire life here. He died last January at 91 years of age. Evidently, it was "an apple a day" that did it because, except toward the end, he never had a sick day in his life.

Cliff figures that the farm will end up with about 1,000 trees to work with. Right now about 600 supply the fresh apples to sell and cider to make.

He points out the distinction between cider and apple juice. Cider is not pasteurized. It's fresh and sweet straight from the apples. Apple juice, on the other hand, is pasteurized and must state so on the label.

As far as his own favorite apple is concerned, he can't be pinned down to one. He likes the Romes, Jonathans, and Russets. For a sweeter apple he favors the Yellow Delicious, but then he also likes the Wealthies early on. He likes apples with a fuller flavor, maybe a little on the sweet side; that is, he likes the slightly sweet ones to eat, "but I really don't like them in the cider." In short, he likes apples.

———————

ROBERT AND CLIFF BORDEAUX

What do you think makes a good cider?

Well, again it's the mixture. Grandpa stressed that to us.
That's sort of the best. A good cider should be very smooth. It
should have a slight sweet taste to it but not overpowering. Not
sickishly sweet, but pleasantly. And it should have a body to it, a
very full flavor. It shouldn't have too much pomace. You shouldn't
feel any coarseness on your tongue from any of the fine-grain
pomace. The real test of that is that after the jug has been sitting
awhile, you can pick it up and look and see if there's a small ring
of pomace under there. And that doesn't happen to us anymore.
And as I say, the antique apples are what I think gives our cider a
unique flavor. In this batch there were some Westfield Seek-No-
Furthers, some Parson's Sweets, very few because those trees are
just starting to come in.

How soon do you recommend that people drink the cider?

We don't put any preservatives in it so it'll only keep about
seven to ten days under refrigeration, maybe a little bit longer,
depending on how cold your refrigerator is, but that's about the
limit—ten days. What happens then is that it starts to working,
starts turning into your harder cider. After the initial ten days or
so, you'll start to notice that it has a natural carbonation in it. The
yeast of the apples is turning to sugar and starting to give it a little
alcohol content. It's a sort of cider champagne at that point. It
really doesn't age well in the plastic jugs that we have now. It ages
best in wood. Of course, Grandpa always used to put up about 150
gallons of cider in the basement and age it over the winter. That's
another science in making hard cider. That's one thing we have
plenty over here—hard cider recipes. Everybody has a favorite.

And you've made some.

Oh, yes, we made some. We actually make an applejack,
which is freezing the cider in the winter and tapping out the core.
It's more of an apple brandy then with quite a bit more strength
because the alcohol is in the middle of the barrel and the water

A good cider should be very smooth. It should have a slight sweet taste to it but not overpowering. . . . And it should have a body to it, a very full flavor.

content is frozen around it. We'll let the rest, after we draw off the applejack, turn to vinegar; people around here like it as a natural vinegar. We give it away to members of the family who like putting up pickles and stuff.

Our wooden barrels are airing out now on the other side of the shed here. The wood helps in the mellowing of the cider and the aging. A charcoal-lined barrel—preferably if there's a little whiskey residue in it—that's a good starter for a hard cider.

ROBERT AND CLIFF BORDEAUX

Some similarities to wine.

Oh, yes. A hard cider is really a strong apple wine. It's hard to say because everybody does their own recipes. A lot of people add sugar or brown sugar. We've been known to put in some honey, but we usually sweeten to taste after it's been aged. Sometimes, depending on the apples, if you have a lot of Delicious in there or a lot of Jonathans or Rome, you'll get a really sweet cider and you won't need to do that. There's a lot of sugar in those apples and it makes a very strong cider. But if you have some that's made out of a lot of Winesaps or Greenings, which are basically a tarter apple, then you'll want to look for something to sweeten it a little bit. Unless you like a drier, tarter wine.

What do you do with the leftover pomace?

We spread a little out on the fields, sort of giving back what we've been taking. Most of it goes out into a pile in the back lots, have it there for the deer. The squirrels burrow through it for the seeds during the winter. Of course, the deer dig for the pomace. It keeps pretty well from this time of year on. They have something for the winter. You go out to the pile and it's all pawed over.

Do you have someone come in and pick the apples to begin the process?

The whole family is usually here. Up to a couple years ago I would handle all the picking myself. Dad would be helping on weekends, and when I was working full time in a boiler room on second shift I would have the entire day so I would come down and pick all day. Four years ago I went back to school to finish my college education. What happens now is that my wife's parents will come up and I'll put a little Tom Sawyer on them like"—Why don't you come up and pick some apples?" They live down in New York City and they like coming up in the country here. Her sisters come up and give a hand and my brother-in-law comes up. He was up last weekend. It was an extra long day for us. We pressed until eight o'clock at night.

Paul Sevigny

Dowsing

Paul Sevigny

Danville, Vermont

The green binder that Paul Sevigny opens on a table is stuffed with records of the more than 800 wells he has found by dowsing. Newspaper articles and letters of testimony and appreciation report success after success with only 35 misses. "A lot better than any well driller!" he says.

Paul has been dowsing for only seven years. His success, enthusiasm, and confidence are so reassuring that he is now, at 63 years of age, president of the American Society of Dowsers headquartered in Danville, Vermont. Organized officially in 1961, the society now has 3,000 members in 52 chapters across the country. Every September a convention is held in Danville, a small town of 1,500 population in winter, 2,500 in summer. The town is set on a high flat stretch of northern Vermont countryside where dowsing has long traditional roots. Last year more than 800 dowsers convened for four days to discuss and share their talents and tributes.

For the last four and a half years, Paul has been dowsing for charities. He's gathered nearly $19,000 for the Boy Scouts, Girl Scouts, 4-H activities, Planned Parenthood, kindergarten school, scholarships for students, and the local library. On his dowsing jobs, he asks that his clients write out checks for the particular charity he's working for that day and then he turns over the money to that particular group. He himself charges nothing, only mileage of 15 cents a mile to cover expenses.

Dowsing is an ancient art. Its most popular image is the forked stick or the Y-rod, as it's now called. Although dowsers use the art to find oil, lost objects, gold, the best-known quest is dowsing for water. That's what Paul, a straightforward, high-energy man, talks about with relish.

———————————

To begin with, what is dowsing exactly? How do you describe it?

I think it's an extension of a sixth sense. You can get as many ideas of what dowsing is as there are dowsers. Some people think it's magnetic action between the water and minerals in the earth. I think it's using the sixth sense that we've always had. In the last 200 years we've just gotten used to turning on the tap; we don't have to look for water. But when our forefathers were going west, every day they always found water for their cattle to drink. Everyone seemed to have the ability then. We just let it stay dormant more or less. I sort of compare it to a wild animal. You don't have to tell a deer where to go for water. It smells around and senses which direction to go for water, and I think that's what we're doing.

Are you saying that it's a matter of tapping our own resources, which we don't normally do in modern life?

Yes. A lot of us agree that we have a lot of gray matter in our brains that we haven't even touched. I think this is part of it.

Is there something that is analogous to dowsing?

Sure. ESP, using your psychic powers. We sort of tie these together.

But there must be something that accounts for a particular dowsing talent that surfaces more in one person than in another. How do you account for something like that?

Again, that goes back to your mind. In order to be a dowser, we have to chase the doubt out of your mind. Once we've done that, you'll be off and running.

DOWSING

Now how do you do that?

Well, we just had a convention and a dowsing school. We had 160 in the school and every one of them had a dowsing reaction before the school ended. First, we told them a couple of stories to get them relaxed. I said we want you to relax and want you to believe that this is going to work. Then we work with them. They hold one end of the stick and we hold the other and then when we get over a vein of water it works. Pretty soon they're doing it and they're getting a reaction.

Among these 160 were there some that had different intensities of reaction? Were there some that had more than others?

Oh, yes, they're all different. It's the same with tennis players and golfers. Some are better than others. Again, it takes a lot of practice and a lot of work to increase your ability to find water fast and be more accurate.

What are some of the changes over the years that happened to you that seemed to bring out the talent more?

When I first started dowsing, I'd just go out in a field and look for a vein of water. It'd be where people wanted to build a house. Maybe they'd want a shallow well, which here in Vermont is less than 12 feet deep. We'd check it out and maybe it'd be 50 or 60 feet deep and that's no good. Now when I go out to find water, I use L-rods [He demonstrates by standing up and walking across the room.] and concentrate and ask myself which direction should I go to find a vein of water. We happen to have a vein of water right through here. Now instead of asking for a vein of water, if I'm looking for a shallow well, I concentrate on something less than 12 feet deep. Now this vein below here is 17½ feet deep. So if I concentrate on something less than 12 feet deep, I get no reaction at all [he doesn't]. If I ask for something under 20 feet, a vein [the rods turn outward parallel to the flow of water].

PAUL SEVIGNY   207

Fantastic. When you concentrate, what exactly are you doing?

Just getting everything out of my mind except what I'm working at.

Are you thinking of 12 feet deep?

No, I'm thinking of a vein of water less than 12 feet deep. I usually use a Y-rod for getting the depth. Of course, you can find this vein using this, too. You can actually hear the squeak in my hands. [He demonstrates again with a nylon Y-rod; the rod squeaks in his hands as it pulls down.] Can't hold it. So if I wanted something about depth, I concentrate on something that can be answered yes or no. If it's yes, it goes down. [It does.] Is it over 10 feet down? Is it over 20 feet deep? [No.] 19? 18? [No.] 17$^1/_2$? [Yes, the stick is pulled downward.]

Amazing.

Yes. Go ahead, try it.

I stand up, take the Y-rod, and hold it on both ends, palms up. I walk across the room and think about a vein of water. The rod pulls in my hands. "There, you're getting a pull," Paul says. I am, I feel it. It's not as strong and startlingly abrupt as what I see in Paul's hands, but it's definitely there.

He comes over and takes one end with his left hand, I take the other end with my right hand. He takes my left hand in his right hand and together we walk across the room. This time the Y-rod pulls down hard and strong. "I can't believe it," I hear myself say.

How long does it take you to find water?

Now it takes me five minutes. I used to spend an hour.

How precise can you get for the depth of a water vein?

Very good. I dowsed for a young man in St. Johnsbury here and his well and his neighbor's both went dry. His neighbor got a well driller and went 600 feet and got a gallon a minute. He needed more water than that. So I went down and found a spot 30 feet from the corner of his house and said right here at 87 feet you'll get more than 15 gallons a minute. He called me up the next Friday and said, I thought you'd like to know about the well. He sounded not too happy, like maybe I'd missed. How'd I make out? Well, you're off a little bit. Oh? How bad? You said we'd get water at 87 feet. We got it at 86.

Was the flow fairly accurate?

Yes. He got 30 gallons a minute. So he was really pleased.

How far can you actually go? Can the quality of the water be involved, too?

Yep. When I'm looking for these wells, I only want potable water, good drinking water. I've dowsed for people with unsuitable water. In one case, I found a vein of good water just 30 feet away. They dug it up and they've been drinking the water six or seven years.

Have you ever been approached by an environmental agency or a similar group to dowse for polluted or toxic water?

Oh, yes, that'd be possible. State agencies are just beginning to get with us now because I've dowsed for judges and law clerks, and for the forestry parks in New Hampshire for water on top of Mount Washington. We think we've got them 70 gallons a minute on Mount Washington, but they've got to get some money to fix the road to get the equipment up the hill. At one time they had a well up there, but someone thought it was for oil and pumped it full of oil and ever since they haven't been able to use it. So they've been spending $35,000 a year hauling it up on the cog railroad.

PAUL SEVIGNY

We did go to Greenfield, Massachusetts, and dowsed for the city of Greenfield and got them 425 gallons a minute. They were going to build a water system at a cost of $15 million. They got two wells for 30,000 dollars. The engineering company that did the drilling had other contracts and they weren't too pleased about that! They tried to pump it dry and they couldn't. They kept taking samples and hoping it would be bad and it wasn't.

Can you develop a latent talent or does it just mature naturally with experience? In other words, can you consciously improve your talent?

Oh, yes, we keep improving all the time. You just learn to relax and take it one step at a time. One thing is that I try to caution people not to go too fast and go off the deep end. It can blow your mind and there are some that have. Like getting into some of these other things like psychic healing and self-hypnosis, things that are pretty far out. It gets kind of touchy, kind of dangerous, unless you do it at a good easy pace and know where you're at, just making sure that you've got a good understanding that you can handle the situation.

You know, everything puts out energy, a chair or a person. We have a lot of people who can see your aura and the colors in your aura and know about you because of these different colors. That's another one of these things that's a little far out if you step a little too fast. You can get yourself muddled up.

Have there been some other unusual agencies or places that you've dowsed? For instance, have you ever found water where you never thought you'd find it?

One example is that the state of Vermont was interested in having a German company purchase some property in Morrisville because it was going to put some 30 people to work. So the state agencies went over and did some percolation tests and everything was OK except that they needed at least 5 gallons per minute of water, which they didn't have on the property. So they hired a geologist from the University of Vermont to come over and the well driller from Morrisville. And then the old German there said, I want a dowser.

DOWSING

Of all the people there none of them believed in dowsing. In order to make him happy, they called me up and asked if I'd come over. I said sure. So we met at a restaurant and had coffee and doughnuts and then headed out to the site. The old college professor said, This is going to be interesting because I've never worked with a dowser before. I said, I've never worked with a geologist before! So the geology professor walked over the site and said, There's no water, absolutely no water. The well driller said we'd probably hit water, but we'd have to go 500 or 600 feet. So I walked over there with my dowsing rods and said, Right here at 86 feet you'll get 4 gallons a minute. If you go down 25 feet more, you'll pick up another 10.

So they looked at me and the professor said, You're wasting your money, and walked off into the sunset. I was their only hope so they said, Well, that's not too far to drill—let's give it a try. At two o'clock the next afternoon the well driller called and said, I thought you'd like to know about the well. I said, Yes, how'd we make out? "We got the four gallons on schedule. The next 25 feet we're pumping 12 gallons and we'll probably get 14." So that one made me feel real good because I was in nothing but negative thoughts. A lot of dowsers think that if you're in among a lot of negative people it's hard to dowse. I felt good because they were looking at me like what kind of a nut is this!

Did you subsequently get in touch with the geologist or he with you?

Oh, yeah, he couldn't believe it.

When you're thinking about the water, are you thinking of its texture, the image of a vein?

I'm thinking about a flow of water going through the earth.

How do you differentiate the depth and the flow of direction?

I like the L-rods because they show me which direction the flow is. You cross the vein and put in a stake. Then you go 100 feet away and cross the vein and put in a stake there. Then you can drill anywhere across that line. Then I use the Y-rods for the depth. It worked so good that I just stuck with them.

PAUL SEVIGNY   211

How does knowing the depth come about?

You concentrate on the direction and then the depth. Again, I'm also concentrating on the depth, too, when I think I want something less than 12 feet deep. I want good drinking water, that's all I want.

Is there a relationship between the intensity of the pull and the depth of the water?

No. I can get just as much pull on it with 5 gallons a minute as with 500. I got one artesian well six miles from here. It's been pumping 105 gallons a minute for six years now and it's got so much pressure we can't cap it off.

The society maintains that everyone is born with dowsing capability and that from any group of 25 adults between two and five will feel a dowsing reaction immediately if they're instructed properly; children are particularly sensitive.

Dowsing in history is reflected in wall paintings and manuscripts. Sixteenth- and seventeenth-century coins depict dowsers at work and this widespread interest and use of dowsers accompanied early American settlers. Then came the rigid scientific mentality and the decline of dowsing in the nineteenth and twentieth centuries.

Nevertheless, the motto of the society—Indago Felix (the fruitful search)—holds sway with some scientists. At the annual convention scientists and scholars of many persuasions have attended and lectured, including professors from the University of Michigan, pharmacists, psychologists, and chemical engineers from Cornell University. The topics have included "Geophysics and Dowsing," "Remote Sensing Through Dowsing," "Dowsing and the Psychology of Intuition," "Traditional Acupuncture, Energy in Our Bodies."

How long after you started dowsing was it that you became so adept at it?

I was dowsing for two years before I had nerve enough to say dig here or drill here. At the time I was in the Vermont legislature and was treasurer for the American Society of Dowsers and I didn't want to screw the society up by making a mistake. So I lacked confidence, and if you lack confidence you'll never be a dowser. Until this old guy, Gordon MacLean, said, Give them the guarantee a well driller gives them. The only guarantee they give is that it's going to cost 8 dollars a foot. They don't know how deep they're going to go or how much water they're going to get or if they're going to get any water. As a matter of fact, I asked a driller how he picked the site if the people didn't say they wanted him to drill here or there. He said he used the beer-cap method. I said, What's the beer-cap method. He said, We pop a beer and wherever the cap lands that's where we dig!

Have you ever had a situation in which people didn't want water in a particular place?

Oh, yes, I divert water veins. This'll crack you up. If someone has water running through their basement, I can pick up where the water is, drive a stake in the ground, whack it and drive the vein in the other direction. I've done that several times. Or I've driven water into wells that were dry. I've done that several times also. Once in June there was a well that was dry. I found a vein 30 feet away and drove it into his well.

I started a rescue squad here 15 years ago; we built a new fire-and-rescue building about three years ago. When we dug the hole for the footing, there were four veins of water running into the hole as fast as you could pump it out. So the fire chief called and said, Hey, Sevigny, can you drive water out of a hole. Come on up here, we need you. This was on a Sunday morning. I went back there 100 feet and picked up each vein and diverted it. Monday the hole was dry and Tuesday they poured the concrete. So I converted 25 of them, standing there shaking their heads! They couldn't believe it.

Why is there such an increase of interest in dowsing in recent times?

Mainly because of publicity. They're taking to us more now. I've had people say, Can you dowse for me, and I'd go out to the house and they'd say, Can you find where water comes into the house. So I'd tell them and say it's right here. And they'd say, Yep, now I know you can do it. You have to prove yourself before they really accept it.

Is there a typical dowser that comes to the convention?

Not really. Back when dowsing first got started, we had mostly old-timers, over 60. Now we're getting a heck of a lot of college kids and high school kids. So it's changed. We get far-out elements. We get nuns, rabbis, carpenters, college professors, MDs. So we've got a mixture. And everyone says it's so nice to be in a town where everyone smiles and says good morning.

One of our board of trustees was a nun and she gets into medical dowsing. She works with physicians in Miami. When they have a patient they can't diagnose, they go to her and she tells them what's wrong and how to treat it. She uses a little plastic instrument and goes through a body-health chart. That's one we have to be careful of because it's against the law in Vermont to practice medicine unless you're an MD.

Are there other aspects like that where dowsing can be applied?

We have a guy who comes here every year who dowses for oil, he does it professionally. We have one guy who hit four wells out of four trys in the West. In California there are a lot looking for minerals and gold.

In an adjoining new solar-heated room called Dowsers Hall, a Register of Recognition hangs on the back wall. It's the hall of fame of dowsers. The famous Henry Gross of Maine is engraved (he was most famous for map dowsing and finding water in Bermuda where no water was supposed to exist). Jack Livingston is listed; he has found 3,000 wells in California so far and dowses as a profession. Paul is slated to have his name engraved.

Most of the dowsers listed are men, but Paul says no difference in talent exists between men and women dowsers. Women are just late coming to the forefront. "As a matter of fact," he says, "we're getting to the point where there's just as many women as men who come to the convention."

Most people call the society headquarters to find a dowser for their well. Normally, the society refers the homeowners back to a local chapter "because we've got a lot of people who are interested in dowsing but they aren't really dowsers."

He says some dowsers who dowse professionally charge at least $50 before they even leave the house. He himself doesn't set any fee and gets anywhere from $10 to $150.

Is there a certain area of the country where there's more interest in dowsing than others?

The Northeast is where most of this got started. We have more chapters in Vermont than anywhere else. We've got four chapters in Florida, five chapters in Ohio. I think the interest in the West Coast is the Oriental influence. We swap journals with the British society of dowsers, New Zealand, Germany, France.

You can measure the effects of dowsing, but is there a way of measuring the process? Do you have any program going that's studying this?

No. We had a professor from North Carolina come up and he wanted to find out if people went into an alpha state when they were dowsing. He put some instruments on me and we went out dowsing and got the same readings as without. So either I was in an alpha state all the time or it didn't register.

What would you tell someone who's interested in dowsing about how to start?

The best way to start is to buy a little booklet and read about it and to go out with someone who's a dowser. I've got three or four people trailing me on every job I go out on. We'll find the same spot. I'll write down the depth of water I've got and they'll

> I used to say, You've got to show me how this damn thing works before I'll believe it'll work. Since I've become a dowser, I've changed my attitude 180 degrees. I believe something'll work until somebody proves that it won't. . . . It's a good attitude. It's an open mind.

tell me what they got and then I'll show them my card. I've got one girl who's been going with me quite a bit lately. She lacked confidence but she's really going now. She writes down the same thing I've already written down. She's a good dowser. She's 23 or 24.

Do dowsers use more or less the same system?

This is why we're more or less convinced it's a mental thing. Some people think that you've got to have an apple crotch. If you believe that's true, this nylon rod isn't going to work. We have one little old lady who comes up from New York City. She has dowsing sneakers! If she hasn't got her sneakers on, she can't dowse. And as long as she believes this, it's going to be true. So that's why we say you've got to chase the doubt out of your mind. All of these instruments are going to work, so they do. But if I didn't believe that plastic or nylon wouldn't work, it wouldn't work.

That's the thing that's kind of interesting. I was in the Air Force for 24 years, a glider pilot in World War II, and in the nuclear weapons program, which is a little bit scientific! I used to say, You've got to show me how this damn thing works before I'll believe it'll work. Since I've become a dowser, I've changed my

216   DOWSING

attitude 180 degrees. I believe something'll work until somebody proves that it won't. I've seen so many damn things happen. It's a good attitude. It's an open mind. This is the reason we can teach children to dowse better than we can adults. They've got an open mind.

You have children who dowse?

Yes, as a matter of fact, we're just getting it written into the Girl Scout book, one of their skills. We're trying to get it into the Boy Scout book next.

You discovered dowsing late in life. Do you think you could have done this when you were 21?

Oh, heck, yes. Sure. If I would have had an open mind!

BILL AND EILEEN ELLIOTT

Living Without Electricity

Bill and Eileen Elliott

Hancock, New Hampshire

No wires lead to the Elliott's home, only a winding path through the woods. No wires mean no electricity, and no electricity means no automatic dishwasher, washing machine, video tape recorder, light bulbs, television, telephone, toaster, refrigerator, and all the other appliances that are part of the modern electrified world. How do the Elliotts survive it all? They're flourishing, and they love it.

It all began when they postponed installing a telephone in their previous house. They soon found that they enjoyed *not* having a telephone and that they could do without many things they had taken as absolutely essential. Then when the time came to build their own house, they could afford only property far beyond access to electricity. They wanted their own home more than electricity, and being the enterprising, set-a-plan-and-achieve-it type that they are, they built their house by hand—literally.

No noisy, gas-exhausting, earth-mangling trucks and machines were used or, for that matter, allowed. They hauled fieldstone by hand for the foundation. They mixed 90 bags of cement by hoe and trough. They hand-sawed their joists, rafters, and beams from timber cut on their own 25 acres. In the end, they moved into their hand-built, 28 × 32-foot, two-level, 1,300-square-foot beautiful home that cost them $12,000 and was paid off in four years.

The eye-opener about the Elliott's home is that this is no log cabin hovel in the dark gloomy forest. No one would ever know that this ordinary looking house is run without electricity. It's a reminder that before electricity people led happy and prosperous lives, and they can today, too.

The Elliotts have adjusted to every difference that no-electric-living implies. They pump their own water, wash clothes by hand-operated machine, light by kerosene Aladdin lamps, listen to radio by battery, cook on wood stoves, have a compost toilet, store food in a cool root cellar and pantry, sweep the floors instead of vacuum, beat eggs by hand instead of electrically, iron with an old-time sadiron instead of by steam.

On top of all this, they consider their quality of life vastly improved over their previous two-car, two-kid suburban style, although Bill is still teaching mathematics at a small nearby college as he did before. At a table overlooking the clean, quiet woods outside, the two of them talk of their relished new life without electricity.

What have you learned most from living without electricity?

Eileen: Seasonal living. And that's going back a long way to what the old-timers did. It's living like our grandparents did. The other day we went to someone's place for dinner. We had eggplant, tomatoes, and a salad. These are the kinds of things we don't do anymore. Right now in March we're down to dealing with onions, carrots, potatoes, squash. It doesn't even enter my mind now, this is how much it's changed, that I can go to the store, buy eggplant, and make moussaka at this time of the year. Moussaka is something we make in the summer. It's the same thing with strawberries and raspberries. We eat volumes of it when it's here.

Bill: It's not just food from ourselves. For instance, we buy citrus from Agway at this time of year. But we'd never dream of buying oranges in the summer or apples now. So it's not just stuff we grow. It's stuff that's appropriate for the climate and time of year.

Eileen: Right now we eat sprout salads instead of lettuce. Or grated carrots.

Are you pulling more and more away from the mainstream?

Eileen: Except that we do go to Boston a lot; we're not becoming hermits in the woods. But our life tends to be more seasonal, that's all. One thing about winter is that it was when the women did their sewing and quilting. I never did that sort of thing before, but I've made a dozen shirts this winter. Now we're starting to do more outdoor work—burning brush, clipping, getting ready to plant in the cold frame. Now I can't stand the thought of going upstairs to sew.

What came first, the rhythm of winter or the idea that now is the time to make shirts?

Eileen: The rhythm of winter. Here I'm all alone. I know that for two or three hours there's not going to be any distractions. I know that if I want to go upstairs and sew for a couple hours, the phone isn't going to ring, nobody's going to come knock on the door. I'm my own limitations. Nothing from the outside world is going to interrupt.

Does this put you off of people? If you know that they're not going to come, therefore, do you hope they never come?

Eileen: No, people become a special thing that you plan for. Because you don't see people when you don't want to see them, you make efforts to see them.

Bill: You select the visits, you have more control over your life. This is the technological age, but how much control do you have over it? How much control do you have over the telephone? It's true that we're going back to how our grandparents lived, as Eileen said, but I see the whole thing as a forging ahead. It's a simple way for more people to live now and in the future. Obviously, we have today a lot of people with all sorts of mental problems, people who can't "get their lives together," one of the terms they use. I think that seasonal living, of getting your body and mind in a seasonal routine, in a sequence, is a comforting thing, a steady constant. I think the people who have the most trouble is that they get up in the morning and in a sense they're free, there's an open slate, but there's no sense of connection with what's going on.

Their teenage sons Tim and Jeff have their own bedroom built separately from the main house. They have their duties like any teenagers, only slightly different. Every member of the family hand-pumps 100 pulls a day to draw water from the spring into the tank upstairs. From there the water flows through the kitchen sink and elsewhere by gravity.

Tim and Jeff also help supply the heating source—wood. At one point the Elliotts had cut, split, and stacked 31 cords (one cord is 4 × 4 × 8 feet). For the house, they figure about an average of five cords of wood to heat, cook, and warm water all year. With about 180 square feet of window panels on the south side, they get 20 degrees worth of free solar heat a day. The entire house is wrapped with 1-inch tongue-and-groove Styrofoam, plus up to 12 inches of fiberglass in the ceiling. The Elliotts use whatever modern materials they need to lead the simple life.

Both Eileen and Bill, who worked in nearby restaurants during the summer, have cooked on a wood stove for many years. "This stove," he says, "is far better than any stove we've ever used."

If you have strawberries in January and October, it's not a big treat when they come around naturally in June and July. Is this part of the rhythm cycle you're talking about?

Eileen: Tim is saying all of a sudden, Gee, I can't wait until we have garden peas and salad. He's saying it with a real eagerness that you wouldn't feel if you were bringing it home from the frozen pea section in the store.

There's also a certain thing you're looking forward to with a lot of anticipation. I mean, you know that when you tap those maple trees that spring is coming. Well, sometimes people have leftover syrup and friends will say, We're not going to tap this year. I could no more *not* tap the trees and go through that muck and mud and snow for syrup. I've *got* to do it. It's just a ritual, it's part of the deal.

Bill: One of the things that was missing in our family life—we've been married now for 19 years—was family rituals. Now there's the first corn harvest, there's the maple syrup, planting the first seeds. On the first snow that covers the ground completely, that's when we have our first brushfire. We go out and have this

The carrots are running out, the potatoes are running out, the beets are gone. It's time to get the jars empty and ready for the next round. So there's a full cycle all-year-round.

gigantic bonfire. It's the first real time it's safe to burn brush. It's night and it's nice and we're getting real work done that needs to be done.

Every part of the year there's something appropriate for the food cycle. This part of the year we eat canned beans, canned corn, because that's what there is. The carrots are running out, the potatoes are running out, the squash is gone, the beets are gone. It's time to get the jars empty and ready for the next round. So there's a full cycle all-year-round.

Is this all part of a spiritual rebirth in any way?

Bill: Without recognizing this seasonal flow and rhythm, without intellectualizing it and talking about it, it's just chores and drudgery. You're just plodding through—"Oh, no, it's maple syrup time, I've got to hang up those buckets. Oh, no, the firewood's gone, we've got to get some more firewood. Oh, no, it's time to dig up the garden again, oh my aching back." All this is not inaccurate, it's hard, difficult, physical work that needs to be done, but if you let yourself get into the natural cycle of things and make yourself think you're doing more than the necessary survival, that if you give it some intellectual, spiritual underpinnings, it helps you go on. I think that's something people are missing, the people who are unfulfilled in their lives. I'm not saying this is the answer for everybody, what we're doing. But I think that people who don't have something like this think their lives are just one plodding chore after another.

What would you change? What would you have done differently at the beginning to get where you are now?

Eileen: I would have liked to have been here a few years sooner. It took us a long time to get here.

Bill: I think we did this at just the right time in our physical lives and at our level of maturity. If we did this ten years earlier at 25 instead of 35, we wouldn't have had a sense of where we fit into the scheme of things. Now it feels everything we did was just right.

Have you been able to adjust to the lack of, say, television? So many people seem to think they need it.

Eileen: Oh, God, what a blessing. I liked *Masterpiece Theatre* on public TV, but it's weird now, it's like television doesn't exist. When I see television and what it's like, I'm not tempted at all.

Bill: We went to a small New Year's Eve party for the first time in 20 years. We enjoyed being there and seeing the people, but what did we do? At quarter to 12 we sat down and watched TV and

New Year's Eve someplace else. I sat there and I just couldn't believe it. With all these people, we had a lot in common, we had great conversations, and we had to watch this plastic stuff on television.

By living here in the woods and pulling away from the outside world, do you find yourself not informed about what's going on?

Bill: Eileen is more informed about Washington than 60 percent of the people, I'm sure.

Eileen: Public radio is wonderful. I listen to about three and a half hours of radio news a day.

What do you read?

Eileen: The ladies in town pass around *The New Yorker, Natural History, National Geographic, Time, Mother Jones, Country Journal, Farmstead.* There are about six people involved. I also belong to a couple of book clubs. We get newsletters from Sierra Club, Amnesty International, Planetary Citizens.

Bill: From my point of view, I'm part of the vanguard of people interested in computer education—learning about computers and helping others to learn about computers. I'm working with that every day at school.

It looks as if you find yourself with one foot in each of two worlds.

Eileen: People say to Bill, You know, you could make better money with computers if you'd just do this and do that. Bill always says to someone who asks that, Will I get my summers? This guy can't believe not wanting to build a career. But to us now time is much more valuable than money. As things progress, we'll need less and less money.

What are you aiming for as far as money and time are concerned?

Eileen: A three-day-a-week job for Bill.

Bill: That's not the ultimate. I think the ultimate is one day a week, in the sense of having to go to the outside world to do something to make money. I don't think we'll ever become self-sufficient in the sense that we'll never need some kind of income. Between September and May I have to work a lot in the outside world, like 40 hours a week, and I don't like that. Then from May until August I'm home virtually all the time. I'd like to spread that out so that I can have more of a sense of this rhythmic flow that Eileen gets.

The Elliotts have found that everything can be done by mechanical means one way or another. Eileen, for example, washes clothes on a James hand washer with wringer. For ten minutes she pumps the washer with one hand and reads a book with the other. It's just one of the many items they bought through *Lehman's Non-Electric Catalog*.

Their refrigerator is a series of shelves downstairs in the cool root cellar where they keep eggs, pasteurized milk, and cheese. Ice cubes they don't have in summer and ice cream they eat right away near the store. Otherwise, they don't really need a refrigerator.

No electricity has many advantages, they stress. For one, the noise level is radically reduced. Vacuum cleaners are not sounding forth and neither are electric mixers, TV commercials, electric razors, clothes washers, dishwashers, or other loud machines.

Says Eileen, "You can have beautiful windows, beautiful plants, use your lovely dishes and set beautiful tables. You don't have to live in a shack in the woods with the outhouse in the back." And Bill adds, "You don't have to be dirty, and you don't have to be hungry."

What do other people react to in what you're doing, how you're living?

Bill: There are three different reactions. People who are like us and on the same wavelength, they're not flabbergasted by what we're doing because they understand. The other extreme is that people have no idea what we're doing. We pass in physical appearance as normal mainstream people. Nobody would suspect that we're doing something out of the ordinary. Then there are some people in the middle. They just can't believe it. People don't believe it until they actually come and see.

That you're not living in some roadside shack.

Eileen: It's always a surprise.

Bill: When we talk about no electricity, heating water on a stove, walking three-quarters of a mile to our car, they imagine a log cabin, a shack. When they come to see us, I think many people are amazed and inspired that it's possible to do it. Not that many people would do it exactly this way, but to see that it's possible to live a good life, a civilized life, and to be able to cut yourself off in ways from whatever mess is out there.

Urban living can be the same for everybody. The same temperature is maintained year-round, you see the same newscast, shop for the same foods throughout the year.

Bill: That's what the lighting problem makes you aware of. I have to get down the lamp and light a match. You don't flick a switch. You light a space where you work, you don't light the whole house and walk around as if it's daytime. It's *night*, it's really night. So not only is there a seasonal cycle, there's a daily cycle.

A frost in July is part of the cycle, not as regular but it does happen, especially in New England. We've always had good-weather and bad-weather projects. Say on a weekend we choose a project that's appropriate for the weather. If it's raining, we can brush. If it's totally miserable being outside, we'll do an inside project. So we're not counting on the weather to be this and thus and you're devastated because it's not right.

Eileen: It used to be like that. I worked in an office and had Fridays off. Twelve Fridays in a row literally it rained or snowed and I'm an outdoor person. Often the weekends were bad, too. That used to really depress me. Now because I don't have that cycle, I can adjust to it. If we get a freak snowstorm, I can enjoy it.

Do you consciously plan to have an indoor project and outdoor project?

Eileen: Yes, we're planners. Oh, yes, we have lists. I can tell you what we're going to do in the winter two years from now.

BILL AND EILEEN ELLIOTT

227

Bill: That's what made this work. We talked incessantly about this for five years, down to the details, making lists, revising and going over and over. We didn't do that idly. I think that's one of the reasons our relationship has been good, too.

Eileen: Learning to set realistic goals and aiming for them and succeeding, that's where it's at.

What would you recommend to people who are looking to do something similar?

Eileen: Step by step, inch by inch.

Bill: You have to know yourself and what you want to accomplish. That doesn't mean copying us. That might mean getting some inspiration as we did from people like Helen and Scott Nearing.

And we do need a social life, but again we're in control. We have an oasis here where we perfectly are in control of our lives. We have the ability to go out there and dip in and say, OK, we're going to dip into the mainstream world, get involved in it when it seems right and then come back here. There's give and take, too, both ways, it's not just take from that world. Because we have this world of ours, we go out there charged. We really have something to offer and something to gain.

The rhythm slows you down, too.

Bill: But it doesn't make you less productive.

Eileen: You're in more touch with what you're doing. It's like kneading bread by hand versus by mixer.

Some people must say that you're not living in the real world.

Bill: You have to go to Los Angeles to be in the real world?

LIVING WITHOUT ELECTRICITY

TREFFLE BOLDUC

Snowshoe Making

Trèfflé Bolduc

Conway, New Hampshire

Trèfflé Bolduc makes and sells snowshoes at his grocery and tourist item store The Snowshoe Center on the eastern end of the Kangamagus Highway, a well-known road that bisects a wild section of the White Mountains. He had been in the building business for about 40 years and didn't want to continue. So one winter day when the snow was about a yard deep outside his store window, he saw two pairs of snowshoes made by Canadian Indians. He looked them over and announced to his wife that he was going to make snowshoes. Knowing that he was always handy with wood, she said she had no doubt that he could.

A friendly, enterprising man, Bolduc set about making snowshoes the best way he could and, to him, that meant the way the Indians make them. "It didn't take me long," he says, "to find out that there was a lot to it." He had to find the proper hides from farmers, remove the hair, get the right wood (white ash, although in some arctic regions birch and black spruce are used because white ash doesn't grow there). Then he had to learn how to soften the wood, use the right mold, how to lace them properly, search out the best harness.

The secret of success and his growing reputation as a maker of tough, old-fashioned designs with lasting modern materials all stems from some of the secrets his Indian friends gave him. Bolduc hints at some of these secrets and tells much about snowshoe making, but it was agreed that no matter how many times he was asked, he wouldn't divulge essential Indian secrets. It is a trust with his Indian friends that he will not break. So with this immutable understanding,

231

he talks about the many other aspects of one of the oldest hand talents of northern snow country.

After you got all this information, how long did it take you to make your first pair?

I experimented from January to March. I had not made one frame and I had worked every day. I tried many different methods of making molds and steaming the wood. There are many different methods and a lot of them are costly if you break the wood. The wood has to be a good-grade wood or you're going to break an awful lot more than you're going to make.

After making them for seven years, I got a bad batch of wood. Three of us must have worked for two months and I don't think we made 10 pair. That was very heartbreaking. It was expensive, it was discouraging, it took a lot out of us. Finally, I solved the problem and went to another method of treating the wood.

What methods solved the problem?

Well, you're getting into personal things now. I told you I was going to limit the information. But I will have to say that dry steam is not good. You have to have a wet steam. I was using dry steam and hoping it would penetrate more into the wood. It might have penetrated more, but the wood was brittle. It'd break.

How long do you have to steam the wood?

That depends on whether or not the wood is green or not when you start. If you start with wood that's dry, then you're going to have to steam a long while and then you're going to have to keep your fingers crossed, hoping that you have luck. But if you get wood that's green, then you don't have to steam so long.

After that you use a mold to shape the wood.

Yes, here's one that's 150 years old. It was found in an attic. Then here's another mold. This one is 125 years old. This one has

232   SNOWSHOE MAKING

a treacherous bend here at the toe. If you haven't got good wood, you'll never make one of those in God's world.

―――――――――

Trèfflé is a man with energy in his words and body. After a few minutes he leads the way from the ice cream section of his store where we're talking to the main section. There he explains the two old molds that form the snowshoe rims before leading the way to the storeroom in the rear.

The room is full of an amazing variety of snowshoes. Some shoes are ancient, all of them are shaped differently. Some have wide toe angles, some are flattened more, some are extremely wide, some narrow.

Large pieces of rawhide are propped against two pairs of Indian-made snowshoes. A long row of snowshoes hangs overhead while others are stacked vertically on the floor. In one corner are some prized snowshoes with important history attached to them.

―――――――――

You have a wonderful collection here.

Well, this is only a small part. I have the largest collection in the world, no doubt about it. I don't mean the most but the different variety. See this one. There's a square toe on that one. Only one tribe makes a square toe. And here's one that was used many, many hundreds of years ago. It's just a couple of boards, like a little ladder. It served the purpose.

Here's a snowshoe that was made by the man who made shoes for the Peary Expedition to the North Pole. Then I've got some from the Stefansson Expedition to the arctic in 1913.

What tribe used the square toe?

I'll never tell you what tribe. Well, it's a Canadian snowshoe. Here's a small one that's used if you're going on a snowmobile and you break down.

Are all these in your collection made of rawhide?

That's all they had in those days, you know. Now, these snowshoes were used by my son when he raced in the world championships in Montreal. Everybody had to use the same length and width snowshoe, about 29 inches by 8 inches, in the 100-meter dash. He came in second in the world. He should have won. That was four years last February at Longueuil.

This is some of the rawhide we use. Now this is a full-grain rawhide, but people stay away from it because it's a lot of hard work; they go to thin stuff like that one. That's why most of the snowshoes made today use split grain. I make the full-grain ones just on order now.

Those shoes over there are made by Eskimos. They're made with sealskin. They're excellent. Those were made on one of the islands in the Bering Strait. It doesn't soak the water like most of the other skins. Most rawhide, once it gets wet, goes all to pieces.

Have you been over to the Alaskan Stefansson Collection at Dartmouth?

Yes, I've been in the museum where the Stefansson diaries are and I went through that to verify this whole story.

I spent some years in the Alaska bush on the Yukon River and . . .

. . . Have you been to Eagle, Alaska?

Yes.

I've got some of my snowshoes there, used by some trappers. Yeah. Now those shoes there are made by the man who made snowshoes for the Peary Expedition. He made 60 pairs. He came from down Maine. I knew his granddaughter very well. He was born in 1866, so that's a day before yesterday. She's 84 years old. She knows all about those snowshoes. These are probably the only snowshoes you'll ever see in the world with a turned-up toe like that. Now Admiral Peary felt that having them like that they wouldn't have so much drag as they would being straight. And he was right. But people don't do that, and I don't do that. It's another chance of breaking the frame.

Those Peary snowshoes are probably 4 feet long.

Well, they're longer than that. They're 56 inches and they're used for open country. Now over here I've got some pictures of the snowshoes we make on Mount McKinley four years ago. These were at 8,500 feet elevation. These were considered the best snowshoes. They were an American group expedition.

Now what happens after the frame is put on the mold?

Then we have to rivet the frame together.

But first, how long does it take to stay on that mold to secure the bend?

That varies. In my case, I try to leave it in there at least a month, but I have some that have been in six months. It isn't necessary to keep them in that long, but I do know that the longer they're in the mold the more they're going to stay in shape. A lot of companies do dry kilns. They take the wood, put it into the mold under tremendous heat and it dries it, but I also have a feeling that it makes it brittle. They break easier. In my case, I stay clear of dry kiln. I tried it in the beginning. I'd rather have it air-dried a long while.

Now you see these snowshoes, you won't see them anywhere in your travels. They're for men up to 300 pounds. Big, heavy frames. Those are for giants. I think I'm the only one in America that makes heavy frames like that. I know some of my Indian friends in Canada do but not in this country. You see that turn-up? Most of the old snowshoes had no turn-up and you trip easily. With this, you can run like a deer and they don't dig in, especially if you're coming down a hill.

The lacing is beautiful work.

Yes, no doubt about it, they do the best in the world artistically, but they are not practical. They're beautiful work, but

. . . I try to leave it in there at least a month, but I have some that have been in six months. . . . I do know that the longer they're in the mold the more they're going to stay in shape.

SNOWSHOE MAKING

they wouldn't last two days here. Our snow is too wet. The rawhide would stretch and break very easily, it's so thin. If you're walking in the woods, a branch would break that very easily. If you're walking in the woods here and you got a lot of snow on top—our snow is on the wet side—it would go through.

Now what do you do after the wood is bent and dried on the mold?

Well, we know that you have to put rivets or rawhide on the ends. Then you take a chisel and make a groove for the crosspieces to go in. Like I always said, every man in the world who makes snowshoes has his own method.

———————

He puts aside the huge oval snowshoes that look like they'd be too small for an elephant. The lacing is thin and intricate. At the end of some shoes, fancy red and blue feathers are attached for a festive look. The Indians make these more for display than for rugged use in the woods.

Trèfflé tells a story of how useful it can be to hand-make snowshoes. Since every maker has his own signature, so to speak, he can tell at a glance which are his own shoes. Several years ago his store was robbed. He went down Maine and accidentally spotted his snowshoes on a shop wall for sale. "Well, I know my snowshoes like nobody else because of my trademark," he says. His trademark is a certain series of two and three twists of rawhide in the middle section of the shoe. "No other man in the world does that," he says. He asked the proprietor if the shoes were for sale and played along as if he were a customer. Then he went for the sheriff who did his duty and got Trèfflé his stolen snowshoes back.

He sells three styles of snowshoes that he makes using Indian techniques. The Beaver Tail is the most popular and easiest to handle. Ten shapes range from 9 × 29 inches for children weighing up to 60 pounds to 14 × 42 inches for adults weighing up to 270 pounds. The Yukon model originated in Alaska and is designed for open country. Because of its narrowness, this style is popular for walking in thick woods. The Otter is a modified bearpaw style used mostly by mountain climbers and snowmobilers. The costs range from $30 to $65 a pair.

What would you tell someone to look for in a good pair of snowshoes? What's the mark of some that will last?

That's a hard question to answer. Now, if you were buying authentic Indian snowshoes, for instance, you don't have any varnish on them. But if you want to buy snowshoes that you want to use, not just look at, then it's very important that you get a light snowshoe. Nothing should be heavier than it has to be, because a pound on your foot is equal to 5 pounds on your shoulders. There are snowshoes that weigh 5 pounds. That's another 25 pounds up top. You get awfully tired. The old snowshoes were like that. I used to work for the forest service. We used to use the old bearpaws. By two o'clock you couldn't drag your feet; you were too tired. So you need a light snowshoe. That's why mine have become so popular. They weigh less than the shoe you have on your foot.

And the lacing has to be so that the snow goes through. That's why I went to nylon. I do a lot of repair, probably more than anybody in this part of the world. I know what makes the rawhide go. It isn't always the snow or the wetness. A lot of times the rodents do an awful job on it; they like the salt, you know. I noticed that the Indians up north started using nylon. That's where I got the idea. I'm not that bright.

Is nylon easier to work than rawhide?

No, it's much harder. People don't realize it. Feel this rawhide shoe. That's firm as a rock. You don't do that just by lacing. Now this nylon is tough, too. I have no woman who can lace snowshoes. It takes a lot of strength to do this. With rawhide, the wetter it is the better it is. So all you've got to do is just lace it. When it's dry it's all done. Put it aside and let it dry. Not so with nylon. But you take nylon and throw the shoes in a river and leave them for a year, they're just as firm as they are now. Put

SNOWSHOE MAKING

those rawhide ones in the water for four hours and they're gone. No, the nylon is much harder to work. It's got to be a man with a good strong hand.

After I learned to make snowshoes from the Huron Indians, I wanted to learn other methods. Whenever I heard of a snowshoe maker, whether he was a white man or an Indian, I would go hundreds of miles to learn his technique. At one Indian place a man made snowshoes the way I did, but he had a unique harness, which I brought back here. I had to change it a little bit because in this country people wear so many different types of boots, whereas up there when you wear snowshoes you wear mukluks.

Yes, in Alaska that's what I wore. I was among the Athabascans.

Well, I have some Athabascan snowshoes. They're quite old, probably 80 years old. Athabascan snowshoes are very nice snowshoes. I don't know about the new ones, but the old ones were well made. Athabascan Indians were the first Indians in North America to make snowshoes. They brought the trade back when they crossed the Bering Straits. They are nomads. In fact, the Indians I'll be staying with in another week, they are nomads. They wander in the subarctic regions. They are not at the mercy of the elements as much now as they used to be. The Canadian government and the Hudson Bay Company watch them very carefully. They fly in and bring flour, sugar, tobacco, ammunition. But these people are quite primitive in many ways.

Are these Hurons?

No, these are the Cree. I'll be visiting many places.

Did you originally go up to the Far North to learn about making snowshoes or for another reason at first?

There was an article in the *National Geographic* about these Indians losing their lands because of the hydroelectric project and their way of life shall be at an end and their snowshoes, which are the best in the world, would also disappear. So I decided to go up there. I saw the people, I saw the way they live. My heart went out for them.

I had heard of Ronnie Loon. He is considered one of the three great snowshoe makers of the world. So I went to see the priest and he couldn't help me, and the manager of the Hudson Bay said he couldn't see how he could help me either. I just accidentally met a 12-year-old boy who could talk some English. "Will you take me over to Ronnie Loon's place?" Yes. Each of the families has a log cabin on the reservation where they stay two months. So we went to Ronnie Loon's and he wasn't there. His wife was there. She gave me kind of the cold shoulder: not interested in selling me any snowshoes. So I went around and then I saw some Indian children. Ah, the Indian children are so cute! They break your heart out. I had a lot of candy and it just dawned on me they might like candy. So after I gave them the candy, she had snowshoes for me. And in a half hour the whole village up there knew I had candy for the children.

These people, I guess, are the finest people I ever met. They don't have a very happy life, they have nothing to be happy about. They can't go anywhere, there's no place they can go, and they're stuck there. So their whole life is their children.

Well, some white people are pretty darned ignorant. That's what happened up there. White people go up there and they laugh at their way of life. But, my God, they're better than the people who laugh at them. Yes, sir. They're certainly tougher than we are. They can stand cold weather better.

Is it because of some of the affection you have for these people that you won't talk in detail of how they make snowshoes?

I won't tell anybody. I've had people tell me that I should write a book, but, no, I would not do it. No, anybody who was good enough to teach me that, no, I wouldn't do it. I never taught a single soul. I have people work for me, four Indians, white people, probably more at times, not a single one of them out of the whole bunch knows the whole operation.

SNOWSHOE MAKING

BERTHA LINDSAY

Shaker Cooking

Eldress Bertha Lindsay

Shaker Village, Canterbury, New Hampshire

Founded in the 1700s in England and known as "The United Society of Believers in Christ's Second Coming," the religious pacifist group was also described as the Shaking Quakers because of their tremblings during worship. In 1776 Ann Lee and her eight followers from England settled in Watervliet, New York, and were considered treasonous because of their pacifist opposition to the War of Independence. Other colonies were established later in New York, New England, Ohio, Kentucky, and Indiana.

In 1792 Shaker converts settled on a farm in Canterbury, New Hampshire, and developed a flourishing community over the years. Their crafts, furniture, architecture, and inventions became known around the country for their directness, simplicity, usefulness, sensibleness, and straightforward beauty—all part of a New England legacy.

Today 22 buildings remain on the welcoming grounds of the Canterbury Village. Eldress Gertrude Soule and Eldress Bertha Lindsay remain, too. Eldress Bertha is 87 years old and is blind now, but she has a brimming memory and likes to talk of the Shaker way of cooking. (Eldress Gertrude likes cooking, too, and confesses that she has not only a sweet tooth but 35 of them!).

Eldress Bertha is a gentle woman with a gentle voice. She leads the way to a room adjoining the parlor and sits at a table where she has waiting two Shaker cookbooks of "tested" recipes. She has talked of Shaker cooking before with others, but she makes this time all fresh and personal again. Her voice is sweet and loving to listen to. She's solicitous about any possible interferences, including their dog Penny who finally settles at our feet. The room has a view across the road to the Shaker village of crisp white buildings where she first arrived in 1905. Time on the large wall clock above us stopped long ago.

———————

Can you remember the very first meal you ever cooked?

Oh my, I don't think I could. That's been over 70 years ago. So I don't believe I could remember that. I remember when I started cooking because at 13 I was making the pies for the family, and at 19 I was making the bread. It was quite a large family then, around 50 or 60 or 75.

That was quite a job.

Of course, we helped each other, but I was responsible. I was appointed to make them. You see, in those days the brothers wanted apple pie just about three times a day—breakfast, dinner, and supper! So if you had apple pie on hand you were all right. But on Saturday we had to make something like 26 pies to cover the weekend because we didn't believe in cooking on Sunday. At 13 the very first pie I made, and this was a contest for our school, was a lemon meringue pie. I *still* make a lemon meringue pie. That's one thing that I can still make pretty good. I always take one orange and two lemons. It kind of softens the taste a little bit. It gives it a nice flavor.

I remember when I started cooking for the hired help and the company who ate down at this building. I was just about 20 then. Sister Josephine thought I would be a good first cook. That meant cooking meats.

What would you point out as some characteristics of Shaker cooking? What would be some of the thinking behind it?

Well, they were always taught to take time to prepare and to start with good seasoning. If you had a pot roast, they would want you to start it with a very good seasoning. Just high enough heat so you could brown it, then lower the heat so it would cook gently.

SHAKER COOKING

Of course, we had our own meat, our own hens, in the earlier days, our own pigs. So the meat was nice and fresh.

That way you knew who handled it and where it came from.

Yes, and how it was fed, too. It was important how it was fed, particularly the pigs. It was good food. It wasn't just all from the kitchen refuse. It was mash in the cold winter seasons. We had to get up and make the hot mash for them, take it out to them. So it was pure and very good food.

With all those pies you must have had an apple orchard.

We had something like 12 apple orchards and a variety of apples so that there were apples for different purposes. We were very fond of Baldwins for pies. We had an apple called the Shenago. We called it the virgin apple because a brother by the name of Virgin planted it here. It's a very dry apple. Makes a very beautiful sifted applesauce that we could use for apple toast or hand pies. Then we would put raisins in for the hand pies. They're little round pies of your dough with the filling, then another piece of dough, press it down, and bake it. Then you could take it right up with your hand. Those were handy for picnics and if we went for pleasure rides. We made a lot of those for the soldiers when the First World War started. I could remember that they were shipped down to Virginia. Then there was the Pippins. And for the early apple we liked the Maiden Blush, the Yellow Transparent. And the Astrakin. That was a beautiful apple, not only for eating but for pies and sauce. For an eating apple we grew a lot of McIntosh.

We had a peach orchard, and at one time peaches between apple trees because the peach trees never lasted as long. We had pears. We ate all we wanted raw and preserved the rest for winter use. Sometimes we sold apples as far as England. Then we had plums, the red June, and the Greengage, the one I love the best. Cherries. We had everything right here.

So fresh they must have been. Was there a favorite dish for the family that you remember?

A favorite dish. Oh my. Well, I'll tell you there was one favorite dish that the Shakers used to make for company. In the early days they served company, tourists that came, they served them the Shaker fish and egg. Now you know in the early days they had a lot of salt codfish because that kept well. So they had aplenty on hand. That was one of the favorites that they served company—the Shaker fish and egg, and boiled apples. It was always a wholesome dinner, with fresh bread and all.

Did you have a cider mill, too, with all those apples growing?

Yes, we had a cider mill. They made their own cider. They served that on the table as long as it lasted sweet. And then it went into barrels to be made into vinegar.

And vegetable gardens?

We had a three-and-a-half-acre piece for our vegetables. It was beautifully laid out. The brothers were very particular. They laid it out in straight rows and this went from north to south back of the houses there. They grew everything. They grew lettuce. The whole length of the garden they had rhubarb, an asparagus bed which was replenished usually every two years. Potatoes, squashes, many of those they sold. The root vegetables because they could be stored away for the winter in sand, the carrots were, to keep them nice. They grew celery. For four years three sisters, and I was one of them, had the vegetable garden to care for entirely. It was the time they called them the victory gardens, through the war years. Well, we raised everything from peanuts to sweet potatoes.

Peanuts! They're difficult to grow here.

The only thing is that we did grow them but we hung them in our garden barn, forgetting entirely that the mice might like them. So the mice ate them! We were hoping to have peanuts to put on the Thanksgiving table as well as sweet potatoes.

Do you remember whether there were some seasons that you couldn't grow enough for some reason or another?

No, we always had plenty, especially tomatoes. I can remember canning over 1,000 quarts of just tomatoes alone. Of

SHAKER COOKING

course, they did have to can a lot of fruits and vegetables for the entire village. And we always shared, because at Christmas and Thanksgiving time we had baskets to take around to the needy. The brothers would carry them around. We always wanted the cooks to make generous provision. We had neighbors who were poor.

For those holidays did you have any special dishes?

Usually the traditional meal, the chickens right on hand or turkeys. At one time we had turkeys but they didn't continue too long. We had a man working for us who knew how to caponize them so we had capons. I wish we had a freezer in those days. We ate as much as we could. We did learn to can chicken, too. And on Thanksgiving we always had turnips. They cooked that a special way; I'll tell you how. There was always aplenty of carrots or beets or whatever. Pumpkin pie or mince pie. We always had a plum pudding, too. Oh, yes.

How did you cook the turnips?

We had a way of cooking it that doesn't seem to hurt people. I cook it a day before, grind it or shift it, whichever is easier. We grind it because that was what we had. Put it into a bag and drain it overnight. That would drain out the extra water in it. I hope it doesn't drain out all the vitamins in it! I wouldn't want to do that. Then the next morning I give it a little extra squeeze to see if there is any more water to come out. Then you put in a little cream or butter, a little salt, and it's *very* good. It doesn't seem to hurt people that way.

———

Tours are given of the Canterbury Shaker Village during the summer and sometimes 18,000 visitors come by in a season. Several of the old buildings are shown and some of the prized old Shaker designs in furniture and architecture as well. Recently, a small restaurant featuring Shaker recipes was opened.

Over the years some famous people have visited Eldress Gertrude and Eldress Bertha. Those included Betsy Palmer, Lloyd Bridges,

Myrna Loy, and Charlie Weaver who arrived in his big Cadillac and had lunch with them downstairs in their dining room.

Eldress Bertha points out some of the favorite Shaker recipes, like Shaker Raised Squash Biscuits, Brandied Fruit Cake, Shaker Fish and Eggs, Vegetable Soup, Shaker Salmon Loaf. They're all contained in a 21-page booklet titled "Shaker Tested Recipes." A picture of Shakers at table is on the cover.

———————————

Did you have certain foods that you avoided?

We tried to avoid too much pork. But other foods it was quite all right.

Did you use foods in a religious way at all?

In a way, we did. Mother Ann gave her followers many counsels and one of them was: Prepare your meals in such a way that those who partake may do so with grateful hearts. They were always very special, that you prepared them well, that you put your best work into cooking so that it would please the eater and the eye, those that looked upon it. We were always taught to plan a meal so that it was colorful. We didn't want it all white or all green or yellow maybe. It had a little red in it maybe. If we didn't have beets on the table, we'd put a little jelly on, or a radish. Something that would bring up the tone. So that color was always stressed for good cooking.

We eat a little with our eyes, don't we?

We do.

What about soups? Did you have special soups that you liked?

Yes, they made quite a few soups. The Shakers had a vegetable soup that was very nice. Of course, people can put in different herbs if they want now. The Shakers did use herbs in the earlier days widely in their cooking and to sell. They grew all types of herbs, not only for the kitchen but for medicines. They pressed them and sold them to the medicinal companies, the pharmacies, you know. Personally, I wasn't as interested in ailments as in cooking.

You chose the right direction all right!

But the Shakers did make a lot of medicines, and they knew just what the different herbs were for. We're trying now to grow herbs again to sell, both medicinal and culinary.

Say, for instance, somebody had a bad cold and was in bed awhile. Was there any particular suggestion for the cook to prepare?

Always chicken broth or chicken soup. Usually it was something hot like that. We used to make our own beef tea. We knew how to get it out of the meat so that it was still palatable, still good for you. A lot of times in the old days they had a special kind of grinder that they put the raw meat in. Then you drank the blood of the creature. It was very good for certain ailments.

The Shakers were very conscious of food and how it should be prepared. So they did do a lot of teaching on cooking. Of course, we didn't stay cooking all the time. I had it for four weeks and then four others would take over the kitchen. We would be under the supervision of trained cooks that were right there with us.

It is proper to treat food well, especially if you have it right here grown by yourself on your own good earth. You'd want to prepare it as best you could.

Yes, everything had to be tasty. I was a good taster! Of course, it spoiled your appetite. It gave me more vitamins than I should have! I think to taste the food is what a cook should do because then you know if it's going to be tasty for others.

And spices? Were they a good part of the kitchen?

We did use spices because, of course, we did mull cider in the cider time of the year. We used cinnamon bark done up in a little bag. They had spice cake and things like that. We didn't overdo on spices, clove especially because that's very bitter. And nutmeg. A little of different things is better than a lot of one. It's an art to learn how to use a little of different spices and herbs. Because you're apt to take up a big pinch. When we say a little pinch, it's a little pinch. That was the way we learned in those days—take a pinch of salt, take a pinch of this and that. It wasn't by a spoon.

That makes sense. You'd want a spice to complement, not overwhelm. Who'd want a cinnamon pie instead of an apple pie?

An apple pie made entirely with nutmeg is very strange to me. I don't care for it. The Shakers always used rose water in their pie. It makes a very delicious flavor, a little rose water.

When you didn't work in the kitchen, what did you do?

We worked on the trades that we made for our livelihood. We made poplar wood boxes, aprons of all kinds, bags of different varieties, stocking dolls, dolls in Shaker costume, Shaker cloaks, Shaker sweaters. So there were enough trades that people could interchange with.

You grew and made so much of your own food. What percentage do you think the family was self-sufficient? How much did you have to get from the outside?

In the early days they must have been 100 percent sufficient because they ground their own flour even. They had a grist mill. You had your different types of flour that you could use right here. We had a little grocery store where we sold surplus. Now we were dependent on getting sugar and molasses and salt, staples like that.

The meals varied every day. If you had a leftover, you were supposed to disguise it in some way so that nobody knew it was a leftover and then make it into something that was palatable. Use all your food, as much as possible.

And you had your own milk products.

We had our own milk and butter until 1918. Then after that we sold the cows. The brothers were not so able to see to that work themselves. We had to have hired workers that weren't so compatible and dependable. So the brothers sold the cows rather than to keep the cows and not do well by them, too, because they were very particular about them.

And cheese?

They had their little cheese house. When I came here, there were wheels of cheese in that cheese house. So they really were independent. Even for the molasses they made barrel staves for barrels that they put molasses into, sent the barrels to the West Indies. Of course, we got molasses in exchange.

Making barrel staves is really quite an art. Now in the kitchen with so many people to cook for, you must have had huge kettles.

They did. Up in our family kitchen, they're still there. We had two large iron kettles. One was quite large, then a small one next to it. Then these were enclosed with brick and had wood fires underneath. You had to learn, of course, to temper that fire underneath so that it wouldn't burn and yet cook well. I can remember a Captain Weldon would come up from Rhode Island with one of the sisters' father and cook chowder in this big kettle. That would be *full* of clam chowder! We were cooking all by fire, but just as soon as something came in that would make the work easier, the brothers would get it for us. So when the electric stoves came in, we had electric stoves.

But in the early days you must have supplied your own wood.

Oh, they did. They chopped about 500 cords. That would go for the heating of our rooms and the cooking.

And did you tap maple trees, too?

We had a special grove of maples and this was about a mile or a mile and a half northeast of our village. It was called the east sugar camp. They had a house there and they would bring the large containers of sap to the house, which was built in such a

way that they could drive right up to the back of the house and
pour the sap right into the kettle. It was built on the side of a hill.
They made hundreds of sugar cakes. This was before my day in
the early 1800s. Oh, it was a great thing to have maple sugar
candy for the St. Paul's boys to come out here. And we had plenty
of syrup. But then the hurricane of '38 blew down those trees like
they were match sticks. And they were huge, too. You could
hardly circle them with your arms.

Through the parlor and across the entrance hall is the gift shop.
In one room Shaker chairs, baskets, boxes, and other artifacts stand
on display. The designs hew to a simplicity that pervades—and em-
anates from—the essentials of Shaker thinking. The adjoining room
is filled with other goods to buy, including a shelf of many different
Shaker cookbooks. Some are better than others, being more authentic,
more Shaker, more tested by Shakers. Eldress Gertrude mentions
that the Pleasant Hill, Kentucky, recipe book is one of the best.
Pleasant Hill is a well-known Shaker community.

Before long we all go downstairs for dinner at noon sharp when
the bell rings. In a clean, pleasant, sparsely furnished room, five of
us sit at table. The setting is colorful and inviting and the food ready
on platters, plates, and bowls—steak, baked potatoes, cauliflower, a
salad of carrots, lettuce, tomatoes, and sprouts. Tea for drinking,
and then comes the Shaker Apple Toast, split rich biscuits layered
with warm cinnamon applesauce and topped with sugar and cream.
It's all very delicious and right.

This recipe from "Shaker Tested Recipes" is a typical lean and
to-the-point example of Shaker ways:

Shaker Vegetable Soup

2 tablespoons barley	1 turnip, small
2 potatoes, medium size, diced	1 stalk celery
1 carrot	

Into 2 quarts of boiling water put 2 tablespoons barley and the
vegetables. Cook until done; season, add 1 teacup sweet cream and
small lump of butter.

Batter for Soup

Combine 1 egg, 1 cup milk, and just enough flour to make a light batter that drops easily off the spoon. Ten minutes before serving soup, while it is still simmering, pour in the batter slowly in a thin stream. It will float around on top, and will have the taste of vermicelli.

Did you eat in family style in the early days?

We ate in family style in our big family dining house. Down in the lower room there is the kitchen, a large kitchen. The dining room had five tables that seated 12 to a table. So we could seat 60 at one sitting. We had a dumb waiter. The cooks would put the food on the table in family style. There were three squares to a table. That meant that four in each little section would partake in that square. It would be all the same, of course. They were long trestle tables. We were always taught to take just what we wanted so as to Shaker your plate! Nothing must be left on your plate. It was better to ask for more than to take it all at once and not be able to eat it all. The brothers and sisters all ate together. Then there would be a separate sitting. There wasn't always room for everybody.

What time did you take your meals?

We have breakfast, dinner, and supper, like country people. At breakfast the cooks usually had to rise by four-thirty to go in and prepare the breakfast. We had oatmeal or cereal of some kind. It wasn't dry cereal; it was always cooked cereal. Sometimes they made muffins or doughnuts. Sometimes it would be mince pie. We would eat around six or six-thirty in those days. The little girls would come in around seven and eat because they had to go to school at eight o'clock. Then at half past eleven the bell would ring that would call the brothers in from the fields and the sisters to tell them to go to their place of residence to get ready for dinner. At ten of twelve the bell would ring to tell them to come

. . . we could seat 60 at one sitting. . . . We were always taught to take just what we wanted so as to Shaker your plate! Nothing must be left on your plate. It was better to ask for more than to take it all at once and not be able to eat it all.

into the house for dinner. Then the dining room bell would ring to come down for dinner all at once. Then we would say grace. This would be at twelve o'clock. We would have supper at around five-thirty.

And the grace. What was said for this?

This was individual grace. It wasn't a prepared one, anything you had to say in unison. It was a silent one. You could say whatever you felt like saying. You could thank the Lord for all the blessings you received, remember those that were in need. You

SHAKER COOKING

were always taught to add that on, to remember those that did not have as much as we did. That was one thing the Shakers never lacked for—food. They always had enough to spare.

Were there other holidays that called for special cooking?

In the early days we had a big family and on holidays we could do whatever we wanted. We had a fancy dinner on New Year's Day, on St. Patrick's, on George Washington Day, on May Day.

Sounds like a good excuse.

It was! It was an excuse to make something special. I can remember we took ice in the pond in March or April when it was beginning to give out. This was in March and I wanted to make a special St. Patrick's Day dinner. The girl working with me went down to the icehouse and gathered all the ice chips and we brought them up and made pistachio ice cream and, of course, colored it green. Then we had everything that was on the table something that had an Irish name. And everything was green that could be! We had a lot of fun.

The seasons of food. Was there a particular season that you liked to cook in than another?

Well, I think autumn was a wonderful time because you had the harvest of the time. You could do so much with the different vegetables and fruits. We had a harvest supper and invited our friends from outside.

Did you have a greenhouse in those days?

They did! Now don't think they didn't! In a different manner though from what you think of a greenhouse because we didn't have them with the glass houses over them. They had a great big deep pit cut out six or eight feet deep. That was lined with cement. Then that was built up with dirt and had glass windows on top. So that was your greenhouse. Then when Mildred and I took over the garden for those four years we wanted to start some things early. So what we did was build a little frame from our cellar window. We had glass windows on that.

Life had its work back then.

They had to work harder. Work is good for people.